DATE DUE

Korea

Korea

BY PATRICIA K. KUMMER

Enchantment of the World
Second Series

Children's Press®

A Division of Scholastic Inc.

New York   Toronto   London   Auckland   Sydney
Mexico City   New Delhi   Hong Kong
Danbury, Connecticut

Frontispiece: Kim Il-sung's birthday celebration, North Korea

Please note: All statistics are as up-to-date as possible at the time of publication.

Book production by Herman Adler Design

Library of Congress Cataloging-in-Publication Data

Kummer, Patricia K.
  Korea / by Patricia K. Kummer.
      v. cm. — (Enchantment of the world. Second series)
  Includes bibliographical references and index.
  ISBN 0-516-24252-0 (alk. paper)
1. Korea—Juvenile literature. 2. Korea (South)—Juvenile literature. 3. Korea (North)—
Juvenile literature. [1. Korea (North) 2. Korea (South)] I. Title. II. Series.
    DS907.4.K85 2004
    951.9—dc22   2003024977

CHILDREN'S PRESS and associated logos are trademarks and or registered
trademarks of Scholastic Library Publishing. SCHOLASTIC and associated logos
are trademarks and or registered trademarks of Scholastic Inc.
1 2 3 4 5 6 7 8 9 10 R 13 12 11 10 09 08 07 06 05 04

Acknowledgments

I would like to thank the Chicago staffs of the (South) Korean Consulate and of the (South) Korean National Tourism Organization for sending me up-to-date statistical information. My thanks are also extended to Elisa Kho, Park Eun-jung, and John Rushing Jr. for providing details about daily life and the cost of goods and services in South Korea. In addition, I extend my special thanks to the staff of the Lisle Library District for giving me access to the library's Asian art collection and to my son Kristopher Kummer for photographing me with these items for the photo of the author at the end of this book.

Cover photo:
Hyangwonjeong
Pavilion, Seoul,
South Korea

Contents

Korean garden

Traditional dress

One Land,
Two Nations

8

Throughout their 5,000-year history, the Korean people have had several names for their land. Perhaps the best-known name is *Joseon*, "Land of the Morning Calm." This name comes from the peaceful way the land looks in the morning. At that time of day, mist hangs over the mountains and trees, providing an almost dreamlike view. Because mountains cover most of the Korean Peninsula, "Land of the Morning Calm" is a name that applies widely.

Despite its nickname, the Korean Peninsula has experienced many events that have hardly been calm. Throughout the centuries, armies from China, Mongolia, Manchuria, and Japan have marched onto the peninsula and tried to conquer the Korean people. Only the Japanese were successful. From 1910 to 1945, Korea was a Japanese colony.

Even during these hard times, the Korean people maintained their spirit and held on to their culture and civilization. This is shown today in the ethnic background of Korea's people. They are almost all ethnic Koreans, with almost no intermarriage with other groups of people. Koreans continue to speak their own language, to

Opposite: **A Korean mountaintop at sunrise**

North Korean residents show pride in their country as they welcome the leaders of both Koreas to the June 2000 Summit in Pyongyang.

practice their traditional music and sports, to wear their unique *hanbok* clothing, and to cook their traditional foods.

The Korean people are also known for passing on their culture. Parts of Chinese culture that were adapted by the Koreans, such as Buddhism, were in turn passed on to Japan. Aspects of Korea's own distinct culture, such as celadon pottery and woodblock printing, were also adapted by the Japanese.

Respected by Their Neighbors

Although several states have invaded Korea, its close neighbors have also had flattering names for the Korean people. One of these names was "People Who Wear White." This name came from the graceful white *hanboks* that commoners wore during the early kingdoms. The hanbok is still worn today. It is honored as a Korean cultural treasure.

The Korean people were also known as "The Courteous People of the East." This name came from the polite way

Korean department store employees greet customers during their pre-opening ritual.

Koreans treated one another, as well as the way they treated foreigners. The Korean people followed a very strict social code of conduct called Confucianism, which originally came from China. Because of this code, everyone knew exactly what was expected of them and where they stood in relationship to everyone else. Korean courtesy is extended in the same way today. For example, Korean subway attendants greet passengers as they exit the trains.

A wooden footbridge, named the "Bridge of No Return," in the demilitarized zone

The Division of Korea

Since 1945, in the aftermath of World War II, the Korean Peninsula has been divided almost in half. In 1948, two countries officially declared their independence and set up their own governments. The two countries are officially known as the Democratic People's Republic of Korea (DPRK) and the Republic of Korea (ROK). By most of the rest of the world, the DPRK is called North Korea, and the ROK is called South Korea. During the Korean War (1950–1953), the two countries fought a civil war. At the end of that war, a demilitarized zone (DMZ) was created, which further separated the two countries. Since that time, the border between the two Koreas has been closed. The Korean people have been kept apart. Perhaps the most cruel result of closing the border was that families were separated and never reunited.

Since 1948, the two Koreas have gone down different roads in almost all aspects of life. North Korea has maintained a communist, one-party government with only two leaders—Kim Il-sung and his son Kim Jong-il. After experiencing the overthrow and assassination of some early leaders, South Korea has gradually become a democratic republic with many political parties. Because of their different styles of government, the economies and societies of the two countries are also quite different. North Korea's economy is totally controlled by the government. It emphasizes building heavy industry to support a large military. South Korea's economy also emphasizes heavy industry, but more recently it has become interested in making consumer goods. North Korea has very little trade with other countries. South Korea's economy depends on international trade.

At this giant statue of Kim Il-sung visitors come to pay respect to the founder of North Korea.

"Kimland" and "The Miracle on the Han River"

The Kims, father and son, have blended their personalities with North Korea's government, economy, and society. For example, after the elder Kim's death, North Korea's constitution was renamed the Kim Il-sung Constitution. Today, gigantic statues of and shrines to the two men stand in North Korea's cities and rural areas. North Koreans look upon the two men as godlike father figures. The people live, work, and even compete in sports in honor of these leaders. They continue to do this even though North Korea is experiencing famine and about 3 million people have died from starvation.

This is all part of the Kims' *juche* philosophy, which promotes a self-reliant North Korea. Through juche, North Korea's people have been cut off from the rest of the world. The news of the world that they receive has been filtered through government censors. Telephone and Internet connections are limited. News that comes from North Korean sources is also censored. The rest of the world knows little about life there. Even when visitors are allowed in North Korea, they can only see certain places. For these reasons, many Western visitors refer to North Korea as "Kimland," an unreal country. Western visitors and scholars also point out, however, that traditional culture is more authentic in North Korea than in the South.

South Korea, on the other hand, is called the "Miracle on the Han River." This refers to the way South Korea's government and people have rebuilt the country since the 1960s. South Korea went from a poor farming country to a rich industrial country. Its economy now ranks twelfth among the other nations of the world. South Korea also has the world's largest percentage of people connected to the Internet by broadband. South Korean students always rank highly on tests given to students in other countries. South Korea has opened its doors to international trade, sports competitions, and cultural events. It hosted the

South Korea's economy thrives as a result of being highly industrialized.

How Korea Is Referred To and the Spelling of Korean Words in This Book

Korea is used to refer to the Korean Peninsula and to the nation or colony of Korea before 1945. After the division of Korea in 1945 and the establishment of independent countries in 1948, Korea is used only to refer to the Korean Peninsula. The Democratic People's Republic of Korea (DPRK) is referred to as North Korea; the Republic of Korea (ROK) is called South Korea.

In 2000, South Korea's government changed the way written Korean is spelled when using the Roman alphabet. For example, the city of Pusan is now written as Busan; Taegu is now spelled Daegu; and Cheju Island is now Jeju Island. North Korea continues to use the former spellings. In this book, the new spelling has been used.

1988 Summer Olympics and the 2002 FIFA World Cup. In 2003, South Korea placed second as the site for the 2010 Winter Olympics. Each year it holds international fashion fairs and film festivals.

Recently, the government of South Korea coined the phrase "Dynamic Korea, the Hub of Asia" as its national motto. The motto expresses South Korea's pride in its economy and its democratic government. It shows that Korea wants to take advantage of its location between China and Japan to become the economic hub of Northeast Asia. However, South Korea's government has been accused of corruption. South Korean workers often hold strikes for better working conditions.

In spite of the many differences between North and South Korea, their governments have conducted talks about reunifying the two countries. Little progress has been made, however. Many Koreans think it might be better to work on reconciling the people of Korea rather than reunifying the governments. In this way, the border could be opened, families could be

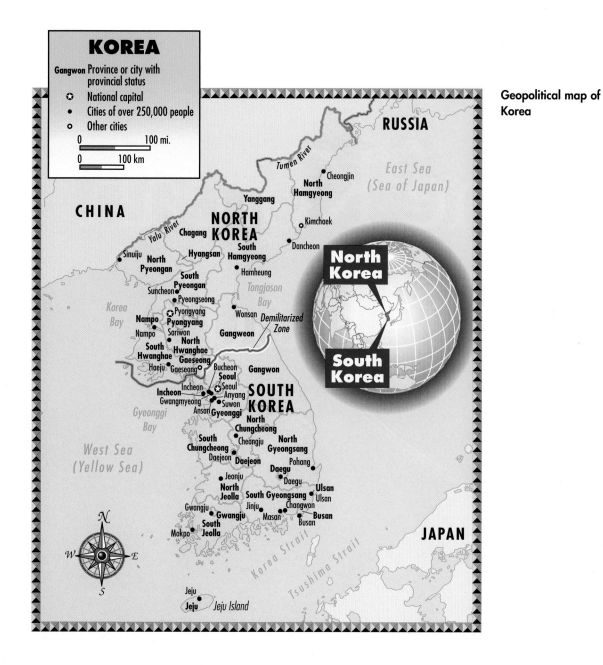

KOREA

Gangwon Province or city with provincial status

✪ National capital
• Cities of over 250,000 people
○ Other cities

0   100 mi.
0   100 km

Geopolitical map of Korea

RUSSIA

CHINA

Tumen River

Cheongjin

North Hamgyeong

East Sea (Sea of Japan)

Yanggang

NORTH KOREA

Kimchaek

Chagang

Dancheon

Sinuiju

North Pyeongan

Hyangsan

South Hamgyeong

Yalu River

South Pyeongan

Hamheung

Suncheon

Pyeongseong

North Korea

Korea Bay

Nampo

Pyongyang
Pyongyang

Tongjoson Bay

Nampo

Sariwon

Wonsan

Demilitarized Zone

North Hwanghae

Gangweon

South Hwanghae

Gaeseong
Gaeseong

South Korea

Haeju

Bucheon
Seoul

Gangwon

Incheon

Seoul

Incheon

Anyang

SOUTH KOREA

Gwangmyeong

Suwon

Ansan

Gyeonggi

Gyeonggi Bay

North Chungcheong

West Sea (Yellow Sea)

South Chungcheong

Cheongju

North Gyeongsang

Daejeon

Daejeon

Pohang

Jeonju

Daegu

Daegu

North Jeolla

South Gyeongsang

Ulsan

Jinju

Changwon

Ulsan

Gwangju

Masan

Busan

Gwangju

Busan

South Jeolla

Mokpo

Korea Strait

Tsushima Strait

JAPAN

Jeju
Jeju *Jeju Island*

reunited, and trade and tourism could take place. The Korean people would then be free to move about the Korean Peninsula again and enjoy their "Land of the Morning Calm."

The Korean Peninsula

THE KOREAN PENINSULA JUTS OFF THE NORTHEASTERN SEC-
tion of the continent of Asia. Many mapmakers say that the
outline of the peninsula looks like a rabbit. The tips of its ears
border on Russia to the northeast. The rest of its ears and face
touch China to the north. China and Russia are the peninsula's only land borders. Since it is a
peninsula, the rest of Korea is bor-
dered by water. To the west, the
rabbit's feet are in the West Sea
(Yellow Sea) facing land in eastern
China. Its back is turned east toward
the East Sea (Sea of Japan). To the
south, its tail is on the Korea Strait,
across from Japan.

The Korean Peninsula and about
3,000 islands cover 85,777 square
miles (222,154 square kilometers) of
land. This is about the size of the state
of Minnesota or the country of
Romania. Within the peninsula,
North Korea takes up 46,540 square
miles (120,538 sq km), a little less
than the state of Mississippi. South
Korea covers 38,328 square miles
(99,268 sq km) and is a bit larger than

Opposite: **Mountainous
North Korea**

**A satellite view of the
Korean Peninsula**

the state of Indiana. The demilitarized zone (DMZ), which divides North Korea and South Korea, makes up the remaining 487 square miles (1,261 sq km) of the peninsula.

Six topographical land regions cover the Korean Peninsula. These regions are almost equally divided between North and South Korea. Most of the Northern Mountains and all of the Northwestern Plain and Eastern Coastal Lowland are found in North Korea. Most of the Central Mountains and all of the Southern Plain and Southwestern Plain are in South Korea.

A Mountainous Land

About 80 percent of North Korea and about 70 percent of South Korea are mountainous. Korea's mountains mainly run down the center of the peninsula in two major land regions—the Northern Mountains and the Central Mountains.

The Northern Mountains region rises over most of North Korea and a small area in South Korea. This is the Korean

The northern mountains of North Korea are covered with dense forest.

Peninsula's largest land region. About one-fourth of North Korea's population is thinly spread throughout the Northern Mountains region. Forests cover the mountains, and rich mineral deposits lie under the land. Two large mountain ranges run north to south through this region. Mount Kwanmo and Mount Buksubaek are the highest peaks in the eastern Hamgyong Range.

Mount Baekdu, the highest point on the Korean Peninsula, rises on the border with China in the Northern Mountains region. This is an extinct volcanic mountain. The lovely Cheonji Lake has formed in the volcano's crater. From Mount Baekdu, the Yalu River flows west into the West Sea and forms part of the peninsula's boundary with China. The Tumen River flows east from Mount Baekdu, forms the rest of the peninsula's boundary with China, turns south to form the border with Russia, and finally empties into the East Sea.

To the south of the Northern Mountains region, the Central Mountains region covers the eastern coast of South Korea and extends along the coast into North Korea. Two main mountain ranges make up this region. The Taebaek Range runs northwest to southeast before it plunges steeply into the East Sea. South Korea's longest rivers, the Nakdong and the Han, begin in the Taebaek Range. Farther inland, the Sobaek Range runs northeast to southwest. Both ranges are heavily forested. South Korean farmers grow crops in small areas of land in the mountain valleys and along the coast. Daejeon, one of South Korea's largest cities, is in this region. More than one-fourth of South Korea's population lives in the Central Mountains.

Korean Peninsula's Geographic Features

Area: 85,777 square miles (222,154 sq km)

Highest Elevation: Mount Baekdu 9,003 feet (2,744 m) above sea level

Lowest Elevation: Sea level along the coast of the East Sea

Longest River: Yalu River, 491 miles (790 km), along the border with China

Largest Lake: Cheonji (Lake of Heaven), 8.7 miles (14 km) around, 1,263 feet (384 m) deep

Largest Island: Jeju Island, 700 square miles (1,800 sq km)

Longest Shared Border: 880 miles (1,416 km) with China

Coastline: 3,050 miles (4,908 km)

Greatest Distance North to South: 670 miles (1,078 km)

Greatest Distance East to West: 320 miles (515 km)

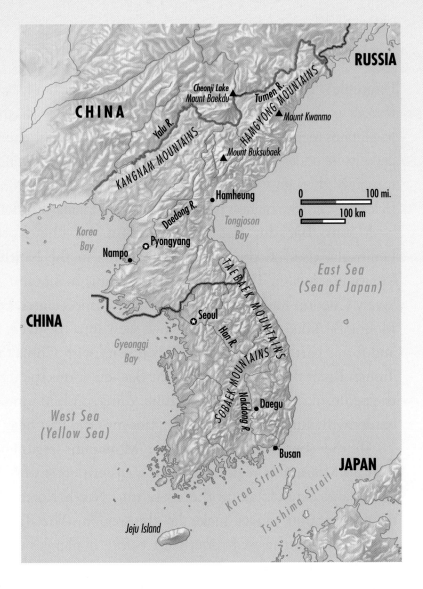

Korea's Lowland Plains

The other 20 to 30 percent of the Korean Peninsula consists of plains, lowlands, and low hills. Several long rivers and short, fast-running streams flow from the mountains across the plains. The peninsula's smallest land region is the Eastern Coastal Lowland, home to more than one-fourth of North

Women harvest rice on the plains of North Korea.

Korea's population. This region is a narrow strip of land along the East Sea. The fish in these coastal waters provide an important source of protein for North Korea's people. West of the coast, plains separated by low hills make up most of the region. These plains are important farmlands. Several of North Korea's largest cities are also found in this region. They include Cheongjin, Hamheung, Kimchaek, and Wonsan.

The Northwestern Plain is located on the other side of the Northern Mountains from the Eastern Coastal Lowland. It lies along North Korea's western coast. The Northwestern Plain is a large area of level land broken up by rolling hills. It has North Korea's best farmland. North Korea's capital city of Pyongyang

North Korea's most fertile land is found on the Northwestern Plain.

sits on the Daedong River in this region. Several other large industrial cities have developed on the Northwestern Plain. They include Nampo, Sinuiju, and Gaeseong. About one-half of North Korea's population lives in this region.

South of the Northwestern Plain lies the Southwestern Plain. This region stretches along all of South Korea's western coast. The level lands and rolling hills here make up an important farming area in South Korea. South Korea's capital and largest city, Seoul, is inland on the Han River. More than one-half of South Koreans live in this region.

East of the Southwestern Plain lies the Southern Plain. It covers the southern tip of the Korean Peninsula. Hundreds of islands lie off the coast of Korea in this region. Many inlets and bays cut into the land along the coast. Inland, much rich farmland is found in this region. Two of South Korea's largest cities, Busan and Daegu, are located on the Southern Plain. Farmers and urban residents in this region make up almost one-fourth of South Korea's population.

Off the southern tip of Korea lie hundreds of islands.

A Look at Korea's Cities

Nampo (below) is North Korea's second-largest city. It is located at the mouth of the Daedong River, about 30 miles (50 km) southwest of Pyongyang. This port city was first opened to trade with other countries in 1897. Today, Nampo is North Korea's major western port. The city's main industries are shipbuilding, glassmaking, and gold and copper refining.

Located on the eastern coast, Hamheung is North Korea's third-largest city. It is also the capital of South Hamgyeong Province. Founded as a government center during the Joseon Dynasty, Hamheung is now a major port on North Korea's east coast. Best known for its hydroelectric power plant, Hamheung is also the leading center of North Korea's chemical industry. Three of the country's colleges are located in Hamheung: the Chemical Industry College, the Chemical Research Institute, and a medical college.

Located at the mouth of the Nakdong River, on the southeast coast, is Busan (above). This is South Korea's second-largest city and the country's largest seaport. The port was opened to Japanese trade in 1876. Busan is also a major industrial center. Shipbuilding, automaking, electronics, and textiles are its main industries. The city's beaches and hot springs draw many tourists each year. Busan has one of the mildest climates on the Korean Peninsula, even though it receives heavy summer rain and an occasional typhoon.

South Korea's third-largest city is Daegu. It is northwest of Busan, almost in the middle of South Korea, and sits on a large plain surrounded by mountains. Attractions range from the Donghwasa Buddhist Temple, built in A.D. 493, to the modern Culture and Arts Center, which opened in 1991. Daegu is also known as the textile and fashion center of South Korea. Every May and October, the Daegu Textile Fashion Festival draws buyers from around the world.

Heavy snow near Seoul makes travel difficult.

Climate

Although Korea is a peninsula, its climate is a continental one. In many ways, Korea's climate is like that in the northern Midwest in the United States. Like that area, Korea has four definite seasons: winter, spring, summer, and fall. Winter starts in December and ends in mid-March. Cold, dry winds blow down the peninsula from northern Asia. January is the coldest month, with average temperatures throughout most of the peninsula below freezing. Winter also brings heavy snow falls, especially in the mountains of northern, central, and eastern Korea. Because the southern coastal areas and Jeju Island have a more tropical climate, the winters there are warmer.

In early spring, yellow dust and sand blow down from China's deserts. By mid-April, Korea begins to warm up. Farmers plant their crops and prepare the fields for the rice crop. Flowers cover the fields and mountains, and cherry blossoms add to the springtime colors.

Summer begins in June and ends in early September. This is Korea's wettest season. Winds called monsoons draw warm, wet air from the southeast Pacific Ocean to Korea. The heaviest rains fall in the south. August is the hottest, most humid month. The southeastern peninsula has the most uncomfortable conditions.

Most Koreans agree that fall is the best season. By then, the heavy summer rains have ended. The temperatures have

Fall is a favorite time of year in Korea.

cooled a bit, and the air is dryer. The landscape turns from green to brilliant yellows, oranges, and reds as the leaves change color.

Typhoon Maemi

In late summer or early fall, southeastern Korea experiences two or three typhoons. Every few years, a severe typhoon hits coastal towns. Typhoons are wind storms that develop over the warm waters of the western Pacific Ocean. When they reach land, they cause great destruction with their strong winds and heavy rains. Like hurricanes, typhoons are given names.

On September 12, 2003, Typhoon Maemi blew through southeastern Korea with 135-mile-per-hour winds. These were the strongest winds ever recorded in Korea. The storm damaged rice crops, tipped over container-lifting cranes in the port of Busan, sank oil tankers, washed out railroad tracks, and destroyed about 2,500 houses. In all, the typhoon caused about $2 million in damages. The storm also caused the deaths of at least 85 people. In the photo below drivers make their way through flooded streets in the city of Busan.

The Natural Environment

K OREANS TAKE GREAT PRIDE IN THEIR NATURAL ENVI-
ronment. Homes, public buildings, and cities are planned with
the environment in mind. These structures are often built facing water, such as a river or the ocean, to catch either warm
air in winter or cool breezes in summer. Buildings and cities
are generally built with a mountain at their back to protect
them from cold winds. Within these homes, buildings, and
cities, relaxing garden areas are set aside. The Korean governments have set aside land for national and provincial parks.
Inside the parks, plants and wild animals are protected.

Opposite: **The Gwallamjeong Pavilion blends with nature in the Secret Garden of Changdeokgung Palace in Seoul.**

Forest preservation is supported by both North and South Korea.

Forests and Flowers

About 4,500 different kinds of plants grow on
the Korean Peninsula. This includes about 160
kinds of trees that are native to Korea. Before
1950, most of the trees in Korea's forests had
been cut down. The wood was used for cooking
and heating fuel. Forests on plains and lowlands
became farmland. Damage from the Korean War
(1950–1953) took many more trees.

Today, forests cover about two-thirds of
South Korea, mainly in the mountains. North
Korea's mountains are also densely forested. The
governments of both countries have sponsored
reforesting programs. As a result, many pine and

scrub oak trees have been planted. Many kinds of pine trees, such as spruce, larch, cedar, and Siberian fir, grace the mountain slopes. Pine trees have played an important role in Korean art and folklore. They are admired for their color, form, fragrance, and ability to resist lightning. Pine leaves and nuts are the main source of food for many birds and other wild animals.

The graceful willow symbolizes peace and beauty in Korea.

The willow and the birch are two other important trees in Korea. Pyongyang is known as the "Willow Capital." A row of willow trees was planted there about 1122 B.C. For Koreans, the willow symbolizes peace and beauty. Birch trees supply some of Korea's hardest wood, which is made into tool handles. Many altars in temples are made of birch. Other hardwood trees found throughout the peninsula include beech, elm, and gingko. Subtropical broadleaf trees still stand along the southern coast and on Jeju Island.

The bamboo plant is an important part of Korea's history. It rises straight and tall in wetlands. Long ago, Koreans planted bamboo to show their loyalty to the king. The bamboo remains a symbol of loyalty and long life. Its straight, graceful form is found in many Korean paintings.

The ginseng plant, which grows underground, boosts the Korean economy. Its roots are believed to improve strength and health. Koreans use the roots in foods, drinks, and medicines. Although ginseng root is now grown commercially, the most powerful roots grow in the wild.

Above left: **The bamboo plant holds importance in Korea and is displayed in Korean art.**

Above right: **Ginseng root**

Many kinds of flowering plants bloom on the peninsula. Azaleas, gentians, and rhododendrons grow in the mountains. Camellias are found on Jeju Island. Cosmos, chrysanthemums, dianthus, fuchsia, and various kinds of lilies grow in meadows. Lotus blossoms are found in ponds. Two popular flowers in North Korea are an orchid called *kimilsungia*, named after Kim Il-sung, and a begonia called *kimjongilia*, for Kim Jong-il. The flowers were developed respectively by an Indonesian and a Japanese horticulturist.

From the blooming lotus (left) to the kimilsungia orchid (right), many flowering plants can be found throughout Korea.

The Rose of Sharon

South Korea's national flower is the rose of Sharon, a white hibiscus with a rose-colored center. In Korean the rose of Sharon is called the *Mugunghwa* because the flower symbolizes *mugung*, or immortality. Because its delicate blooms survive in harsh weather, the rose of Sharon stands for the Korean people's courage, which has seen them through many centuries of hardships.

Wildlife

The damage done to Korea's forests in the mid-1900s also destroyed the habitats of many Korean animals. At one time, antelopes, bears, leopards, lynx, and Siberian tigers roamed Korea's forests and mountains. Although most scientists believe the great cats are now extinct in Korea, a few might still exist in remote areas of North Korea. In recent years, a few brown bears have been spotted on the peninsula. Today, the most common large animals are wild boars, deer, and an occasional wolf. Other animals include badgers, foxes,

Common throughout Korea are the wild boar (left) and the badger (right).

martens, northern pika, water shrews, muskrats, and Manchurian weasels. The Amur goral is an interesting animal. This white animal is part antelope and part goat. Ponies run wild on Jeju Island. Their ancestors were left behind by Mongolian invaders in the early 1300s.

Bird-watchers have recorded 422 kinds of birds in Korea. About fifty of these birds are native to the peninsula. The other 320 just pass through. The endangered Manchurian crane and Tristram woodpecker have been named living national treasures. Herons, cranes, and other waterbirds nest along Korea's coastline and in rice paddies. Game birds include the ring-necked pheasant and many kinds of ducks and geese. Other winged creatures include butterflies. Korea's forests provide a home to the *Papho maacki*. This swallowtail butterfly is native to Korea. The markings on its wings provide camouflage among the trees.

Herons are a common sight along Korea's marshes and coasts.

Many animals also live in Korea's coastal waters. The largest of these are sharks, squid, and octopuses. More common are shellfish such as abalone, clams, oysters, scallops, and shrimp. Pearl-producing oysters are found along the southern coast. Pollack, filefish, and sardines are also found along the peninsula.

Octopuses are found in Korean waters.

National Parks and Gardens

Korea has a long tradition of protecting the environment. Conservation laws were passed as early as the A.D. 500s. For centuries, monks guarded the natural areas around their monasteries. Today, many of the peninsula's national parks are located at the sites of ancient monasteries. North Korea has more than thirty protected areas, including about ten national parks and several reserves and special protected areas. South Korea has at least twenty national parks and about the same number of provincial parks. Korea's oldest and largest trees are

The Jindo Dog

Although North Korea and South Korea do not have national animals, the South Korean government named the Jindo dog as a natural monument. This dog is native to Jindo Island. It is known for its loyalty and keen senses. With white or yellow fur, the Jindo has short pointed ears, a thick neck, and a bushy, curly tail.

A Peek at Korea's National Parks

Mount Baekdu Biosphere Reserve is on Korea's border with China. Highlights of the reserve include large areas of forest that has never been cut, the highest peak on the peninsula, and Lake Cheonji, one of the world's deepest mountain lakes.

Mount Myohyang National Park (above) is in southwestern North Korea. The main highlight of this park is the Pohyon Temple Complex, which dates back to A.D. 1044. Another feature is the 3.5-mile-long (6-km) Ryongmun Big Cave. Its large caverns are named

Mountain Peak of the Great Leader Kim Il-sung and the Juche Cavern. The International Friendship Exhibition, which glorifies Kim Il-sung and his son Kim Jong-il, is found in the park's deep forest.

Mount Seorak National Park stands in far northeastern South Korea. Known as South Korea's most rugged and most beautiful national park, it has about 5 million visitors each year. Mount Seorak ("Snow Peak Mountain") has thick forests of broadleaf and pine trees and is the home of many deer and a few bears.

found in these protected areas. Most of the peninsula's wild animals make their homes in the national parks and reserves. Because Korea is a mountainous land, most of the protected areas are centered around well-known peaks. South Korea also has three coastal national parks, however. Tadohae Marine National Park is the country's largest park. It covers several islands along the southern and southwestern coast.

In Korea, gardens must look natural. Water, rocks, plants, and wood are included in their design.

Yeomiji Botanical Gardens houses more than 2,000 plants and trees including semitropical plants.

In Korea's national parks, the natural environment is protected and not changed. Korea's many private and public gardens also look like natural areas. People have worked hard to make them appear this way. In fact, Koreans want their gardens to look more natural than nature. The basic elements for a Korean garden include water, rocks, wood, and plants. Koreans can trace their interest in gardens back to about 30 B.C. The best preserved of Korea's early gardens is Anapji pond in Gyeongju, South Korea, which was built about A.D. 670. Large rocks line the bank of this huge pond. Several wooden pavilions share the shoreline with rows of willow trees. One of South Korea's newer gardens is the Yeomiji Botanical Garden on the southwestern coast of Jeju Island. This is a huge indoor complex. About 2,000 kinds of plants are arranged in traditional Korean gardens, as well as in Japanese, French, and Italian styles. In Pyongyang, North Korea, the Central Botanical Garden has special hothouses named after the country's two leaders.

Five Thousand Years of History

KOREANS SPEAK OF THEIR HISTORY AS BEING FIVE THOU-
sand years long. This is an estimated length of time because no
historic event is connected to a date as far back as 3000 B.C.
However, archaeologists have found that people moved from
the Altaic Mountain area of Central Asia to the Korean
Peninsula at about that time. These people hunted, fished,
and gathered food. Later, they began farming. These early
people held a belief system known as shamanism. It is from
these people that today's Korean people trace their ancestry
and spoken language. Historians and archaeologists have also
found evidence that people were living on the Korean
Peninsula as early as 28,000 B.C. These people are know as
Paleoasians. Tools and pottery from these earlier people have
been found near the present-day cities of Pyongyang, Seoul,
and Busan. It is thought that the migrants from Central Asia
pushed the Paleoasians from the peninsula to other lands in
the Pacific.

Opposite: **Prehistoric life along the Han River**

Legendary Founder of Korea

According to legend, Dangun is the founder of Korea and the father of the Korean people. His father was Hwanung, the son of the ruler of Heaven. His mother had once been a bear before Hwanung transformed her into a human being. The legend says that Dangun was born near Mount Baekdu. In 2333 B.C., Dangun moved to Pyongyang, where he built a walled city and established the ancient Joseon Kingdom. Dangun is supposed to have lived more than 1,000 years before he became a mountain god in far northern Korea. Today, Koreans celebrate October 3 as National Foundation Day. This is the day Dangun is believed to have founded ancient Joseon in 2333 B.C. From that year, Koreans mark 5,000 years of history.

There was an ancient Joseon Kingdom. Whether it was founded by Dangun is another question. Ancient Joseon was located between the Liao River in southern Manchuria and the Daedong River in present-day North Korea. Large clans built other walled towns and eventually became part of the Ancient Joseon Kingdom. Warriors in ancient Joseon used bronze and iron daggers and spears. Farmers had iron hoes, plowshares, and sickles. These tools helped farmers increase their rice crop production. During this time, the *ondol* method of providing heat under floors was developed. In this method, heat from the kitchen stove was passed from room to room under the floorboards.

Ancient Joseon had close contacts with China. China, however, did not consider Joseon to be an equal, independent country. In 109 B.C., the emperor of China's Han Dynasty decided to expand his empire and attacked Ancient Joseon. In 108 B.C., the capital at Pyongyang fell to the Han.

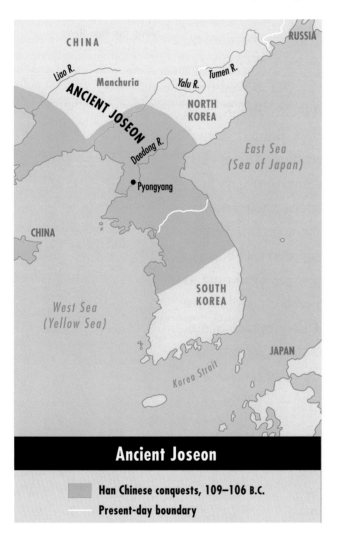

Ancient Joseon

Han Chinese conquests, 109–106 B.C.

Present-day boundary

China set up four territories in Joseon. Each territory sent yearly tribute in the form of crops and other goods to China. In exchange for tribute, China protected the territories from invaders. From this contact with China, three important influences came to the people of the Korean Peninsula throughout several hundred years: the Chinese written language, Buddhism, and Confucianism. Because the Koreans had no written language, they began to use the Chinese writing system of ideographic characters. The Buddhist religion appealed to the Koreans with its emphasis on loyalty to the state and compassion to all. The Confucian code for organizing society and government enabled Korea's rulers to maintain order in their kingdoms.

Ancient Joseon was invaded by China's army in 109 B.C.

Built in the seventh century, Cheomseongdae is the world's earliest known observatory. Its technical structure and position relates to astronomical positions.

Little by little, China lost direct control of the four Korean territories. By 37 B.C., the southernmost of China's Korean territories had been unified as the Goguryeo Kingdom. It extended from the Liao River to just south of present-day Seoul. About this time, two kingdoms were formed in southern Korea: Silla in the southeast and Baekje in the southwest. Goguryeo, Silla, and Baekje are known as the Three Kingdoms.

During the A.D. 300s, Goguryeo adopted Buddhism and established a Confucian academy. By the 500s, the other two kingdoms also had adopted Buddhism and Confucianism. Silla made its own advances in science and technology. During the mid-600s, Cheomseongdae, the world's first astronomical observatory, was built in the Silla capital at Gyeongju. The world's first woodblock printing also occurred there. All three kingdoms sent tribute to China. They also fought with one another. Eventually, Silla formed an alliance with China's Tang Dynasty. With Tang help, Silla conquered Baekje in 660 and Goguryeo in 668. A few years later, Silla pushed the Tang army from Pyongyang.

For 250 years, Unified Silla (668–918) controlled the Korean Peninsula from Pyongyang to the southern tip. Land north of Pyongyang was controlled by the Barhae Kingdom. This kingdom had been set up by Korean people who had pulled away from Goguryeo before 668. Silla continued to send tribute to China, and in 735, China recognized Silla as Korea's only kingdom. The kings of the Silla Dynasty ruled from their capital in Gyeongju. They set up a strict social and political order called the bone-rank system, which was based on an aristocratic family's rank. A person's or family's bone rank determined their home's size; their clothing type and color; and the number of horses, carriages, and other goods they could own. Most peasant farmers owned their land. The main crops were rice and hemp. Farmers paid taxes and performed free labor for the government, such as building irrigation canals and roads.

During the 700s, the Silla Dynasty reached the height of its power and wealth. The great Buddhist temples

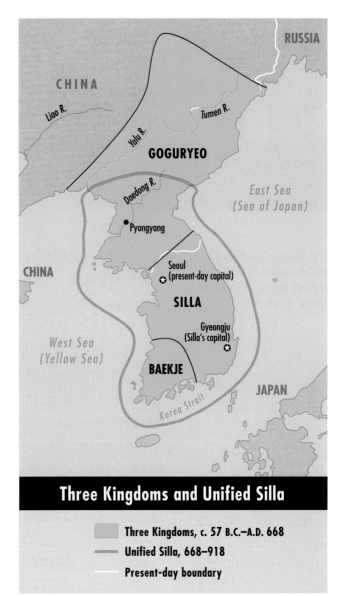

Three Kingdoms and Unified Silla

Three Kingdoms, c. 57 B.C.–A.D. 668

Unified Silla, 668–918

Present-day boundary

The Bulguksa, which means Buddha Land according to legend, is one of Korea's oldest temples.

Bulguksa and the Seokguram Grotto were built. Korea's largest bronze temple bells were cast during those years. These bells have a unique dome shape. The largest is the Emille Bell. It measures 7.5 feet (2.27 m) across the bottom and 11 feet (3.3 m) high.

In the 800s, Silla began to break apart. Aristocrats began to chip away at the kings' power. Peasants who were treated unfairly rebelled. In 918, Wang Geon, an aristocratic general, established a new dynasty with its capital at Gaeseong. He called it the Goryeo (Koryo) dynasty. The name for Korea comes from this dynasty's name. In 935, Wang received the formal surrender of the last Silla king. He also married a woman from the Silla royal family. Wang reunited the peninsula and extended the northern border to the mouth of the Yalu River. In 1044, a later ruler had a great wall built from the Yalu southeast to the East Sea.

Korean Kingdoms, Dynasties, and Governments

Ancient Joseon Kingdom	?–108 B.C.
The Three Kingdoms (Goguryeo, Baekje, Silla)	About 57 B.C.–A.D 668
Unified Silla Kingdom or Silla Dynasty	668–918
Goryeo Dynasty	918–1392
Joseon Dynasty	1392–1910
Colony of Japan	1910–1945
"Temporary" Division of the Peninsula	1945–1948
Republic of Korea (South Korea)	August 1948–present
Democratic People's Republic of Korea (North Korea)	September 1948–present

The Mongol Empire spread as its armies conquered the Korean Peninsula.

Goryeo kings brought Confucian scholars into the government. Knowledge rather than aristocratic rank became important as a way to advance oneself. Buddhism again became the official religion. Cultural achievements under the Goryeo include the development of inlaid designs in celadon porcelain, the printing of the entire works of Buddhist teaching with more than 81,000 woodblocks, and in 1234, the world's first use of moveable metal type.

In 1231, the Mongol invasion of the Korean Peninsula was the beginning of the end of the Goryeo Dynasty. Genghis Khan, the Mongol chief, had conquered China, and his grandson, Kublai Khan, had established the Yuan Dynasty (1260–1368) there. Then, the Mongols turned to Korea and completed that conquest in 1259. In 1274 and 1281, the

Mongols forced the Koreans to help with two failed attempts to invade Japan. By 1382, the Ming, a native Chinese dynasty (1368–1644), had overthrown the Mongol Yuans, and the Goryeo king had removed the Mongols from Korea.

Korea's social structure had fallen apart under the Mongols. Korean aristocrats had gained control of the farmland. Peasant farmers had become serfs or tenants. Artisans and other middle-class people had become slaves. Some of these people had been given in tribute to the Mongols along with ginseng, horses, gold, and silver.

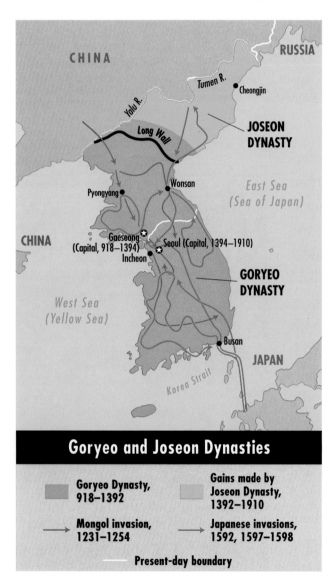

Goryeo and Joseon Dynasties

Goryeo Dynasty, 918–1392

Gains made by Joseon Dynasty, 1392–1910

Mongol invasion, 1231–1254

Japanese invasions, 1592, 1597–1598

Present-day boundary

The Joseon Dynasty

With the Mongols gone and Korea in a state of decay, General Yi Seong-gye seized power in Gaeseong. In 1392, Yi was proclaimed king and established the Joseon Dynasty. He moved the capital to Seoul and began construction of a 10.5-mile (17-km) wall around the city. Yi replaced Buddhism with Confucianism as the state religion. Sons of aristocratic landowners attended Confucian schools to prepare for civil-service examinations that would admit them to government positions. Yi placed all of Korea's land under his control and parceled it out to military leaders and government officials.

Yi's grandson, King Sejong (1397–1450), is regarded as Korea's greatest ruler. He extended the Korean border in the north to the Yalu and Tumen rivers. This is North Korea's northern border today. He encouraged inventions such as the rain gauge, the use of moveable type, and the creation of a Korean alphabet called hangeul. However, the Confucian system that Sejong and later Joseon kings promoted created a strict social system with little chance for advancement. It also discouraged the development of industry and trade.

King Sejong the Great ruled during the Golden Age of Korea. This time was one of great cultural and educational advances.

In 1592, the Japanese began a campaign to attack Ming China by going through Korea. They landed at Busan and captured Seoul and most of the peninsula. The Ming Chinese united with armies of Korean landowners, peasants, and slaves to force the Japanese out. A second unsuccessful attack began in 1597. The attacks greatly weakened Korea and its government. Thousands of people died, land was destroyed, fewer crops grew, and taxes decreased.

After recovering from the Japanese invasions, Korea was invaded from the north by the Manchus of Manchuria in 1627

Turtle Ships

During the Japanese invasion in 1592, Admiral Yi Sun-sin (1545–1598), pictured below, developed the world's first ironclad ships. They were called turtle ships for their protective metal shell. The enemies' spears and arrows bounced off the ships. Yi's few ships intercepted and destroyed hundreds of Japanese supply ships in the Korea Strait. This helped save Korea. In 1597, the Japanese attacked again and once more Yi's navy defeated them. Yi was killed during one of the battles. Today, Yi Sun-sin is considered one of Korea's great heroes. A festival is held in his honor every spring.

and 1636. The Joseon Dynasty surrendered to the Manchus after many Koreans were killed and much land was destroyed. Korea then sent tribute to the Manchus. In 1644, the Manchus overthrew the Ming Dynasty in China and set up the Qing Dynasty. In response to the Japanese and Manchu invasions, the Joseon Dynasty closed Korea off to all countries except China. The kings built a high wooden palisade fence across Korea's northern border. Korea became known as the Hermit Kingdom.

Between the 1640s and 1876, Korea remained isolated from the rest of the world. However, Korean officials met Western scholars in China during tribute missions. These officials brought back books about the Catholic religion and scientific discoveries, as well as inventions such as telescopes and alarm clocks. At the same time in Korea, a group of scholars were promoting *sirhak*, or "practical learning." These scholars were opposed to Confucian learning. Instead, they promoted social equality and the welfare of all people. They also worked on improvements for agriculture.

In 1876, Japan forced the Joseon Dynasty to open Korea's doors. In that year, Korea signed the Ganghwa Treaty, which opened the ports of Busan, Incheon, and Wonsan to Japanese trade. In 1882, the United States and Korea signed a treaty for trade and diplomatic relations. Within the next few years, France, Germany, Great Britain, Italy, and Russia also signed treaties with Korea. Government representatives, businesspeople, and religious missionaries from those countries came to Korea. Groups from Japan and the Western countries worked to make doing business easier in Korea. They built Korea's first railroads, which connected Busan to Seoul to Incheon. Telegraph and telephone lines also connected Korea's main cities. Missionaries built hospitals, schools, and universities.

By the end of the 1800s, the Joseon Dynasty was very weak. Korea's neighbors—China, Japan, and Russia—tried to gain control of the peninsula. From 1894 to 1895, Japan fought China for influence in Korea. Japan won and forced China to recognize Korea as an independent country. For the first time since 108 B.C. Korea no longer had to pay tribute to China. Then, in 1904 and 1905, Japan and Russia fought for control of Korea. Again, Japan won, and Russia recognized Japan's influence

In May 1905, Japan crushed the Russian fleet in the Korea Strait, asserting its power over Korea.

over Korea. Later in 1905, Japan made a treaty with King Kojong. Korea came under Japan's protection. In 1910, Japan forced the last Joseon king, Sungjong, to sign a treaty making Korea a colony of Japan. The king was forced to give up his throne and to move to Japan.

Japan Rules Korea

From 1910 to 1945, Japan ruled Korea as a colony. This meant that Korea and its people existed for the benefit of Japan. Many Japanese farmers and fishers came to work in Korea. They were given Korean farmland and rights to fish in Korean waters. Japan divided the peninsula into a southern agricultural area and a northern industrial and mining area.

Japan wanted the Koreans to become Japanese. The Koreans could not become Japanese citizens, however. The Korean spoken and written language was replaced with Japanese. Korean language and history were no longer taught in the schools. Korean names were even replaced with Japanese ones. In reaction to these policies, thousands of Koreans left their homeland and immigrated to China, Russia, and the Hawaiian Islands.

On March 1, 1919, Korean nationalists signed a declaration of independence that was read in the streets of Seoul. For several weeks, thousands of people throughout Korea took part in peaceful demonstrations for independence from Japan. The Japanese put down the movement and killed about 7,000 Koreans. As a result, Korean nationalists fled to Shanghai, China, or to the newly formed Soviet Union, which had been known as Russia until 1917. In Shanghai, the nationalists set up the Provisional Government of the Republic of Korea. Rhee Syngman (1875–1965) was elected president of this government in exile.

In the 1930s, Japan used Korea as a staging area for its invasion of Manchuria and then China. Korean crops were used to feed the Japanese army. Korean boys and men were forced to serve in the army. Other Koreans were taken to Japan to work on farms or in factories. Only in recent years has it come to light that about 200,000 Korean women were forced to be prostitutes for the Japanese army.

In 1939, World War II broke out in Europe. Before the war started, Japan had formed an alliance with Germany and Italy. These countries were known as the Axis Powers. Great Britain, France, and the Soviet Union, known as the Allies, opposed the Axis Powers. In 1941, the United States joined the Allies when Japan attacked Pearl Harbor in the U.S.-controlled Hawaiian Islands. During World War II, life became even harder for the Korean people under Japanese rule. At this time, Kim Il-sung rose as a leader of the Korean communist nationalists. He led many raids against the Japanese from bases in China and the Soviet Union.

After the United States dropped atomic bombs on Japan, the Japanese surrendered and World War II ended in August 1945. The Allies had agreed to divide the Korean Peninsula at the 38th

Rhee Syngman, president of Korea's government in exile

Koreans cheer as U.S. troops march through Seoul in 1945.

parallel temporarily and to govern it as a trusteeship. Soviet troops marched into northern Korea and accepted the surrender of Japanese troops there. The United States accepted the surrender of Japanese troops in southern Korea.

A Divided Korea and the Korean War

The Soviet Union immediately closed off Korea at the 38th parallel and placed Korean communists in positions of power. Kim Il-sung was elected secretary of the North Korean Communist Party and became chairman of the provisional government. In the south, the government was run by the U.S. military. In 1946, the Representative Democratic Council was set up with Rhee Syngman as the chairman. In 1948,

Below left: **Koreans set up a portrait of Soviet Union leader Josef Stalin in preparation for a parade in Soviet-dominated North Korea.**

Below right: **A young Kim Il-sung became North Korea's first premier**

United Nations–supervised elections were to take place in the north and the south. The result was to be an elected National Assembly for a united Korea. The Soviets refused to allow the UN into the north. In the south, elections were held in May 1948, and a National Assembly was elected. The National Assembly wrote a constitution and formed a government. Rhee Syngman was elected president of South Korea in July 1948, and in August the Republic of Korea was proclaimed. In the north, the Supreme People's Assembly was formed, and Kim Il-sung was appointed as premier. In September 1948, the Democratic People's Republic of Korea was established in the north. In 1949, the Soviet Union and the United States withdrew their troops from the Korean Peninsula.

CHINA

SOVIET UNION

Chinese intervention, Oct. 1950

Yalu R.

UN maximum advance, Nov. 2, 1950

East Sea (Sea of Japan)

Iwon

Landing of U.S. 7 Division, Oct. 26, 1950

Pyongyang

Demilitarized Zone

Armistice line, July 27, 1953

38th Parallel

CHINA

Panmunjom

Incheon ● Seoul

Chinese and North Korean maximum advance, Jan. 25, 1951

Landing of U.S. X Corps, Sept. 15, 1950

North Korean maximum advance, Sept. 15, 1950

West Sea (Yellow Sea)

Busan

JAPAN

Korea Strait

Korean War, 1950–1953

——— Communist fronts   ⟶ Communist advances

——— United Nations fronts   ⟶ United Nations advances

In June 1950, Kim Il-sung began an invasion of South Korea. Kim's goal was to reunify Korea under his control. The United States responded by having the UN organize troops from several countries. Within a few months, the troops had pushed the North Korean army as far as the Yalu River. Then

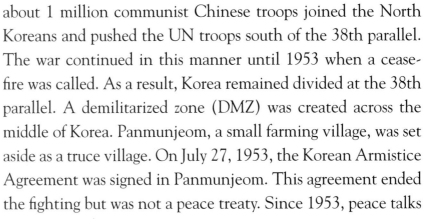

Above left: **UN troops fire shells into communist positions during the Korean War.**

Above right: **The signing of the Korean Armistice Agreement ended the three-year Korean conflict.**

Bitter fighting between UN troops and the North Korean army demolished this street in Seoul.

about 1 million communist Chinese troops joined the North Koreans and pushed the UN troops south of the 38th parallel. The war continued in this manner until 1953 when a cease-fire was called. As a result, Korea remained divided at the 38th parallel. A demilitarized zone (DMZ) was created across the middle of Korea. Panmunjeom, a small farming village, was set aside as a truce village. On July 27, 1953, the Korean Armistice Agreement was signed in Panmunjeom. This agreement ended the fighting but was not a peace treaty. Since 1953, peace talks have occasionally taken place in Panmunjeom.

At the end of the Korean War, both North and South Korea were in ruins. Farmlands had been trampled, forests destroyed, and railroads and highways torn up. Cities, including Seoul, were flattened. Millions of Koreans were homeless and jobless. At least another 2 million Korean soldiers and civilians on both sides had been killed during the war. Some estimates range as high as 5 million deaths. Both countries had many years of rebuilding ahead of them.

At first, North Korea's economy pulled quickly ahead of South Korea's. The north had most of the peninsula's mineral deposits and had been highly industrialized before the war. The peninsula's only hydroelectric power plant was in the North. In addition, North Korea received aid from China and the Soviet Union. Kim Il-sung's one-man rule was able to accomplish much very quickly. His government built schools, hospitals, parks, and other facilities that improved the daily life of most North Koreans.

Kim instituted his *juche* philosophy of self-reliance as the north's only political belief. This meant that the North Koreans were to be politically, militarily, and economically self-supporting. The people were to obey the Supreme Leader (Kim) no matter what. Before Kim's death in 1994, he had prepared his son Kim Jong-il to succeed him in power. This was in keeping with previous Korean dynasties. However, it was the first and only time in a communist country that a son had followed his father as the country's leader. Today, Kim Jong-il holds more power over his people than any other leader in the world. As a lasting tribute, Kim Il-sung was proclaimed "eternal president" in 1998. That ended the office of president in North Korea. No one else can hold that title.

In the late 1980s, North Korea's economy began to decline as trade with China and the Soviet Union decreased. Then, a series of floods followed by droughts hit the country in the 1990s. This brought about years of famine from which the country is still trying to recover. During these economic troubles,

President Park Chung-hee led South Korea's economic boom but abused his political power.

North Korea's government continued to build its military and arsenal of weapons, including nuclear weapons.

Until 1960, Rhee Syngman led South Korea's governments. These governments were weak and corrupt, and Rhee's time in office was marked by many student demonstrations. Few improvements had been made to the economy since 1953. In 1960, Rhee stepped down and elections were held for a new government. Economic problems continued, however. In May 1961, a military coup led by Park Chung-hee overthrew the government. In 1963, Park was elected president by the electoral college. Park began a series of five-year plans, and South Korea's economy boomed. Multi-lane highways and railroads were built to connect major cities. Emphasis was placed on building steel mills and cement plants and on encouraging shipbuilding and the new auto industry. By the late 1970s, South Korea was known as the "Miracle on the Han." President Park used his power to suppress dissent by jailing many of his opponents. He rewrote the constitution so that he could be re-elected any number of times and hold unlimited power. Finally, members of his own government had had enough. In 1979, the head of the National Security Force assassinated Park.

Park was followed as president by Choi Kyu-hah. When the government delayed constitutional reforms, such as direct election of the president, many South Koreans took part in demonstrations. This resulted in the military taking control of the government. The most violent demonstrations took place in the city of Gwangju. There, the military killed hundreds of demonstrators in what is known as the Gwangju Massacre.

This incident caused Choi to resign. He was followed as president by Chun Doo-hwan, who was actually responsible for the massacre. Although the economy continued to improve, students demonstrated for a more democratic constitution. Finally, in October 1987, a new constitution that allowed direct election of the president was approved. In December, the first direct election of a South Korean president was held. Every five years since then, a new president has been elected.

In December 2002, Roh Moo-hyun, a political outsider, was overwhelmingly voted into office as president. When he took office in February 2003, Roh established three goals for his government: democracy for the people, a society of balanced development, and an era of peace and prosperity in Northeast Asia. Within a few months, however, his administration was rocked by a campaign fundraising scandal. Roh's campaign had accepted $9.7 million in illegal contributions. Roh almost resigned from office over this matter. Then, in March 2004, the National Assembly impeached Roh and suspended him from office for violating election laws. Roh had openly supported a political party during the campaign for the April 15, 2004, elections to the National Assembly. South Korea's president is supposed to remain neutral during National Assembly campaigns. In May 2004, the Constitutional Court overturned Roh's impeachment and completely reinstated him as president.

In 2004, Roh Moo-hyun's political status was strengthened when he was reinstated as president after being impeached.

Communist Dictatorship, Democratic Republic

56

A S IN MANY ASPECTS OF LIFE ON THE KOREAN PENIN-
sula, the governments of the two countries provide a study in
contrasts. Both North Korea and South Korea have constitutions that guarantee freedom of speech, press, and religion.
They also call for the election of government leaders. The people in North Korea have no real freedom, however, and they
can only vote for candidates from Korea's communist party. In
other words, North Korea is a communist dictatorship.

From 1948 to 1987, strong presidents limited freedom and
representative government in South Korea. They rewrote
South Korea's constitution nine times, giving themselves
unlimited powers and unlimited terms of office. In 1987, when
the constitution was last amended, South Korea finally
achieved true representative democracy. The constitution
now greatly limits the powers of the president, strengthens the
power of the legislature, and protects human rights. However,
South Korea's government has been rocked by political scan-
dals, including bribery and vote fraud.

Opposite: **South Korean
students wave reunification
flags during the Liberation
Day festival.**

The National Governments of the Two Koreas

In North Korea, government power is supposed to rest with a
one-house legislature called the Supreme People's Assembly
(SPA). Its 687 members are elected every five years from a sin-
gle list of candidates. The SPA meets only a few days each
year. At that time, it approves decisions already made by the

North Korea's parliament building houses the Supreme People's Assembly.

Korean Workers' Party (KWP). All of North Korea's leaders must belong to the KWP. Real control of the government in North Korea lies with leaders of the KWP and the military. The chairman of the National Defense Commission heads both of these groups. The chairman rules the country through the State Administrative Council. North Korea's judicial system consists of the Central Court, provincial courts, and people's courts at the city and county levels. Judges and justices in the judicial system must also be members of the KWP.

Homes of Two Presidents

South Korea's president works and lives in the Blue House. This building's name comes from its blue ceramic tile roof.

The Presidential Palace in North Korea has been renamed the Kumsusan Memorial Palace. Kim Il-sung was the only president to live there. Now, it is his final resting place. Kim's embalmed body is on display there.

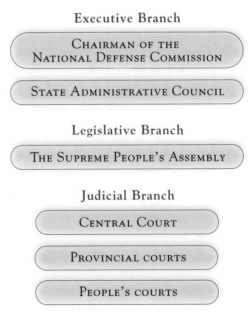

NATIONAL GOVERNMENT OF NORTH KOREA

Executive Branch

CHAIRMAN OF THE NATIONAL DEFENSE COMMISSION

STATE ADMINISTRATIVE COUNCIL

Legislative Branch

THE SUPREME PEOPLE'S ASSEMBLY

Judicial Branch

CENTRAL COURT

PROVINCIAL COURTS

PEOPLE'S COURTS

The three branches of South Korea's national government—executive, legislative, and judicial—are set up to check and balance one another. The president heads the executive branch and represents the country. South Korea's presidents are limited to one five-year term and are elected directly by the people. The last election was held in December 2002. The president is commander-in-chief of the armed forces and can declare war. The president also proposes laws to the legislature; carries out existing laws; appoints members to the State Council; appoints a prime minister who directs the ministries, or departments, of the government; and appoints the chief justice of the Supreme Court.

South Korea's legislature, called the National Assembly, is made up of 273 members. Legislators are elected to four-year terms and can be reelected. The most recent election was held in April 2004. The legislature meets in the National Assembly Building. This building has space set aside for legislators from North Korea should reunification occur. The main duty of the

NATIONAL GOVERNMENT OF SOUTH KOREA

Executive Branch

PRESIDENT

STATE COUNCIL

PRIME MINISTER

ADMINISTRATIVE MINISTRIES

Legislative Branch

NATIONAL ASSEMBLY WITH 16 STANDING COMMITTEES

Judicial Branch

SUPREME COURT

HIGH COURTS

DISTRICT COURTS

FAMILY COURT

ADMINISTRATIVE COURT

CONSTITUTIONAL COURT

South Korea's National
Assembly in session

National Assembly is to pass
the laws for the nation.
Other duties include approv-
ing the national budget,
declaring war, and making
motions to impeach, or
remove, the president or
other elected officers. The
National Assembly has sixteen standing committees that cor-
respond to the ministries.

The Supreme Court is South Korea's highest court. It
hears appeals from lower courts. The high courts, in turn, hear
appeals from civil and criminal cases decided in district courts,
the family court, and the administrative court. The
Constitutional Court works to safeguard the constitution and
to protect the people's rights. This court also holds impeach-
ment trials upon a motion by the National Assembly.

South Korea's Constitutional
Court holds a hearing. In
2004, this court decided to
reinstate President Roh after
the National Assembly had
impeached him.

Political Leaders of the North and South

As of 2004, Kim Jong-il (1942–present), pictured below, held complete power in North Korea as chairman of the National Defense Commission, general secretary of the KWP, and supreme commander of the People's Army. He officially succeeded to power in 1997, three years after his father Kim Il-sung's death. Kim Jong-il makes few speeches and travels little inside or outside of North Korea. He surrounds himself with loyal supporters who do not dare contradict him. He made one major public appearance at the June 2000 Summit in Pyongyang with South Korean president Kim Dae-jung. Although Kim Jong-il is called "Dear Leader," he will probably be remembered for ruling the country during a great famine and for taunting South Korea, the United States, and other countries with threats of making nuclear weapons.

Kim Dae-jung (1925–present), shown above, president of South Korea (1997–2002), is known as a peacemaker. He is a Catholic who was born on a small island in southern Korea. Kim was a good student who completed a master's degree in economics at Gyunghee University in Seoul. Kim's rise to power was a long struggle. As a member of the National Assembly, he was imprisoned by Park Chung-hee in 1961. After that, he faced five death sentences, six years of imprisonment, and ten years in exile or under house arrest. Kim ran for president unsuccessfully in 1971, 1987, and 1992. Coming to power during the great Asian financial crisis, Kim restored South Korea's economy. He is best known for his "Sunshine Policy" toward North Korea, which culminated in the first meeting of the two countries' leaders at the June 2000 Summit. Later that year, he was awarded the Nobel Peace Prize for his work to promote democracy and to reconcile with North Korea.

Two Flags for Two Countries

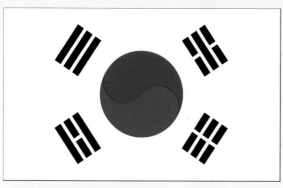

South Korea's flag (above) is called the *Taegeukgi* because of the *taegeuk* circle in the middle. The swirls in the circle represent the balance of forces in the universe: red stands for positive forces, or *yang*; blue, for passive forces, or *eum*. The sets of broken and unbroken lines in the corners also represent balance. The three unbroken lines at the top left stand for heaven; in the opposite corner of the flag, three broken lines stand for earth. The lines in the lower left corner represent fire; the lines in the upper right corner represent water. The purity of the Korean people and their peace-loving spirit is symbolized by the flag's white background. The

Taegeukgi was first proclaimed as Korea's flag in 1883, during the Joseon Dynasty. It is sometimes called the world's most philosophical flag.

The symbols on North Korea's flag (below) have political and historical meanings. The two blue bands stand for the unity of the Korean people with people around the world in the fight for independence, peace, and friendship. The two white bands represent Korea's ancient culture and heroic people. Korea's homogeneous population is symbolized by the white circle. The red band represents the patriotism of people who died fighting to reunite Korea during the Korean War. The red star stands for the revolutionary ideas of Kim Il-sung.

Local Government

North and South Korea have nine provinces (*do*) each for a total of eighteen provinces on the peninsula. The provinces in turn are divided into cities (*si*) and counties (*gun*). In addition, there are six provincial-level cities (*jikhalsi*) in South Korea: Seoul, Busan, Daegu, Daejon, Gwangju, and Incheon. North Korea has four such cities: Pyongyang, Cheongjin, Gaeseong, and Nampo.

People's assemblies and committees are elected at all levels of North Korea's local governments. They carry out the regulations of the KWP for all political, economic, and cultural activities. In South Korea, local government was disbanded between 1961 and 1991. In 1991, the first local assembly elections were held. They were followed in 1995 by elections for provincial governors and city mayors. These local governments manage public property and assess and collect local taxes.

The People's Rights

People in both North and South Korea have the right to vote. All citizens 17 years and older have that right in North Korea. In South Korea, citizens 20 years and older have universal suffrage. The constitutions of both countries grant many other human and civil rights. South Koreans, however, have struggled to attain full exercise of these rights. Not until 1987 were free multiparty elections held. Before that time, people who opposed the government were imprisoned or held under house arrest. Some chose or were forced to leave the country.

South Koreans cast their vote during the presidential election in 2002.

North Koreans really have no rights at all. The press is regulated by the government; free speech is not allowed. There is no freedom of religion, even though some temples remain open with a few monks as show for tourists. North Koreans cannot leave the country or freely move about within it. For this reason, few North Koreans are allowed to buy cars or bicycles—even if they could afford such transportation. About 200,000 political prisoners are held in isolated camps throughout North Korea. Entire families are imprisoned together. They undergo re-education until they die or convince the prison officials that they have become faithful followers of the *juche* and Kim Jong-il.

Military Forces and Foreign Affairs

The Korean Peninsula has been called the scariest place in the world by some visitors. The reputation comes from the size of the two countries' armies and North Korea's ability to build nuclear weapons. North Korea has the world's fourth-largest military force, with about 1.1 million soldiers, sailors, and air crews. Another 4.7 million people are in the reserves, with an additional 3.5 million in a civil brigade called Red Guards. All males between the ages of 16 and 28 are required to serve between 3 and 10 years of military duty. North Korea spends an estimated 12 to 44 percent of its gross national product on its military. The average for other countries is about 2.6 percent.

North Korean soldiers march at Kim Il-sung Square in Pyongyang during a ceremony to mark North Korea's fifty-fifth anniversary.

Because of the large military force north of the DMZ, South Korea maintains an army, navy, and air force of about 683,000 troops. An additional 3 million people are in the reserves, and another 6.3 million serve in the Civilian Defense Corps. This costs the government about 2.8 percent of its gross national product. Between age 19 and 30, all males must serve between 26 and 30 months in military service. South Korean men can-

The 55th Armed Forces Day ceremony in South Korea.

not leave the country until they have taken care of this duty. Because the United States has been South Korea's main ally since 1953, about 37,140 U.S. troops remain stationed in South Korea.

Because North Korea believes in the *juche* idea of self-reliance, the country again became a "Hermit Kingdom" in 1953 isolated from most of the world. Its only allies were the communist countries of China and the Soviet Union. When China began trade and diplomatic relations with South Korea and after the Soviet Union collapsed, North Korea became truly isolated. In the 1990s, North Korea began reaching out. In 1991, both North and South Korea were admitted as members of the UN. The two Koreas had begun moving closer together in 1970, when they had recognized each other's government. Between 1971 and 1973, North and South Korea held talks about reunification and about bringing together families that had been separated by the Korean War. Into the 1980s, however, no progress had been made. In 1991, the two countries came to further agreements on reconciliation, nonaggression, and cooperation. The main problem that remains between North Korea and the rest of the world is its threats to produce nuclear weapons. Early in 2003, North Korea pulled out of the Nuclear Non-Proliferation Treaty. In October 2003, North Korea announced that it actually was making nuclear weapons. These actions make the Korean Peninsula one of the world's unstable areas.

Seoul and Pyongyang: Did You Know This?

Seoul (above) is located on the Han River in northwestern South Korea and stands 282 feet (86 m) above sea level. Residents of Seoul experience average daily temperatures of 23 degrees Fahrenheit (–5 degrees Celsius) in January and 75°F (24°C) in July. About 50 inches (126 centimeters) of rain fall on the city each year. The city's official bird is the magpie and the official flower is the forsythia. Founded in 1392 as the capital of the Joseon Dynasty, Seoul is now the peninsula's largest city, with about 9,891,000 people. It is South Korea's commercial, cultural, and industrial center. Seoul's important industries include food processing and textiles. Cultural attractions include sections of the original city walls and four of its gates, five Joseon palaces (Gyeongbokgung,

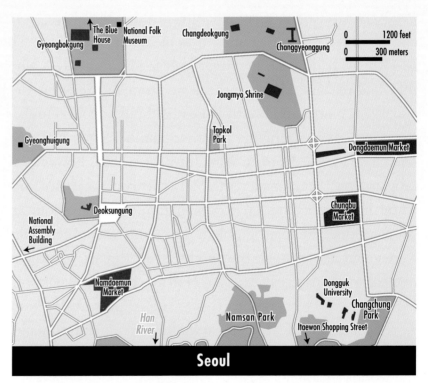

Gyeonghuigung, Changdeokgung, Changgyeonggung, and Deoksugung), the National Museum of Korea, the National Folk Museum of Korea, the Jogyesa Temple, and the Jongmyo Shrine. Shopping takes place at the Dongdaemun Market, the Namdaemun Market, and Itaewon Shopping Street.

Pyongyang (right), meaning "flat land," is located on the Daedong River in southwestern North Korea and sits at 89 feet (27 m) above sea level. Average temperatures range from 18°F (−8°C) in Janury to 75°F (24°C) in July. About 36 inches (92 cm) of rain falls on Pyongyang each year. According to legend, Pyongyang was founded in 2333 B.C. by Dangun. In A.D. 427, the city became the capital of the Goguryeo Kingdom. Today, Pyongyang is North Korea's largest city with a population of about 3,136,000. Pyongyang is the political, economic, cultural, and educational center of the country. Main industries include chemical plants, iron and steel mills, sugar refineries, textile mills, and factories that process food and make electrical equipment. Major cultural attractions include monuments to Kim Il-sung, such as two of the old city gates, the Tower of the Juche Idea, the huge bronze statue of Kim Il-sung, and the Korean Revolution Museum.

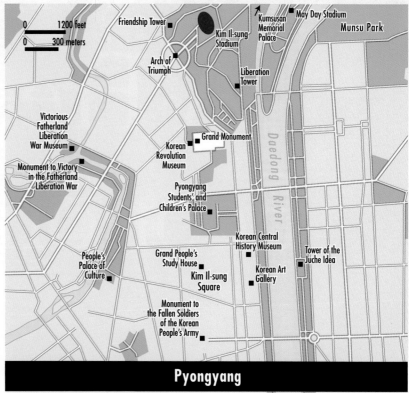

Pyongyang

A Controlled Economy, A Free Economy

THE ECONOMIES OF THE TWO KOREAS ARE TOTALLY DIFferent from each other. North Korea's economy is completely controlled by the government. The government owns all the land, factories, and housing. It determines what and how much is grown, produced, exported, and imported. South Korea, on the other hand, has a free-enterprise, capitalistic economy similar to that of the United States. Farmers own their land. Groups of people own and run companies, factories, banks, and a stock market. Individuals own their own homes.

During the 1990s, both countries experienced economic crises. In the mid-1990s, floods and droughts ruined North Korea's crops. This led to a famine throughout the country. Because the government was slow to react and to ask for help from other countries, it is estimated that at least 3 million people died from starvation. The North Korean government denies this, placing the number of dead only in the thousands. By 2004, North Korea was still trying to recover from the famine.

In 1997, a financial crisis hit most countries in Asia, including South Korea. The value of South Korea's currency dropped and the stock market fell, causing the economy to collapse. Many businesses closed, fewer goods were produced, and thousands of people lost their jobs. South Korea's government quickly stepped in, arranged for loans from the International Monetary Fund, and made changes in how

Opposite: **South Korea's economy is one of free enterprise. Here a South Korean looks at the stock index board in Seoul.**

The Two Koreas' *Wons*

The official unit of currency in both North and South Korea is called the *won* (W). In North Korea, a won equals 100 *jon*. The exchange rate in U.S. dollars is not the same for both countries, however. In North Korea, U.S. $1 equals W151; in South Korea, U.S. $1 equals W1,165.

Each country has its own coins and banknotes. North Korea's banknotes come in W1, W5, W10, W50, and W100 denominations; its coins are the W1, W5, W10, W50, and 1 jon. South Korea's banknotes are the W1,000, W5,000, and W10,000; its coins are the W100 and W500.

The banknotes of both North and South Korea are decorated with colorful pictures of people and places that have historical, political, or cultural importance, as shown below.

South Korea Note	Color	Front of Note	Back of Note
W1,000	Purple	Yi Hwang, Confucian scholar	Confucian Academy
W5,000	Brown	Yi I, Confucian scholar	Yi I's birthplace
W10,000 (below)	Green	King Sejon and a water clock	Gyeonghoeru Pavilion

North Korea Note	Color	Front of Note	Back of Note
W5	Blue	Students	A palace
W10	Brown	A worker	A bridge
W50	Red-brown	Businessman, woman worker	A forested mountain
W100	Red	Kim Il-sung, the "Great Leader"	A Korean village

business was conducted. By 2000, the country's economy was once again booming, and South Korea the world's twelfth-largest economy.

Farming and Fishing

About 30 percent of North Korean workers and 12 percent of South Korean workers are farmers. Rice is the main crop in both countries. North Korea also raises large amounts of potatoes, corn, barley, and wheat. South Korea has large crops of vegetables such as cabbage, onions, and sweet potatoes. Fruit crops of melons, pears, persimmons, and peaches are also plentiful in the south. The Daegu area is know for its apples. The warm climate of Jeju Island produces oranges and pineapples. Farmers in both countries raise beef and dairy cattle, pigs, hogs, and chickens.

Here women are planting rice, the primary crop for both Koreas.

The diving women of Jeju Island are a celebrated part of the island's heritage.

Fishing makes up a small but important part of both countries' economies. Women on Jeju Island are famous harvesters of the sea. They are known as free divers because they go underwater to great depths without breathing equipment. These women gather kelp, seaweed, and oysters. Other fish and shellfish in southern waters include anchovies, mackerel, mussels, and octopus. Along the peninsula's east coast, abalone, cod, king crab, pollack, and squid are plentiful. Waters off the west coast provide abalone, blue crab, lobsters, shrimp, and surf clams. Much of the catch from both countries is exported.

What North Korea Grows, Makes, and Mines

Agriculture (2001 est.)

Rice	2,060,000 metric tons
Potatoes	1,882,000 metric tons
Corn	1,482,000 metric tons

Manufacturing (2000 est.)

Cement	15,000,000 metric tons
Crude steel	1,000,000 metric tons
Pig iron	250,000 metric tons

Mining (2001 est.)

Magnesite	1,000,000 metric tons
Iron ore	700,000 metric tons
Phosphate rock	350,000 metric tons

What South Korea Grows, Makes, and Mines

Agriculture (2001 est.)

Rice	7,453,000 metric tons
Cabbage	3,420,200 metric tons
Dry onions	1,073,700 metric tons

Manufacturing (2001 est.)

Cement	52,046,000 metric tons
Finished steel	49,072,000 metric tons
Synthetic resin	9,017,000 metric tons

Mining (2001 est.)

Zinc concentrate	5,129,000 metric tons
Copper ore	226,000 metric tons
Iron ore	195,000 metric tons

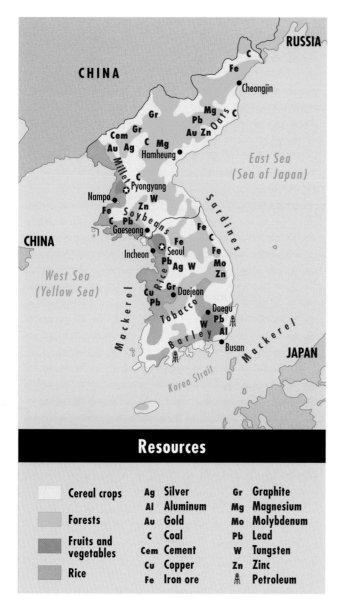

Resources

▢	Cereal crops	Ag	Silver	
		Al	Aluminum	
▢	Forests	Au	Gold	
		C	Coal	
▢	Fruits and vegetables	Cem	Cement	
		Cu	Copper	
▢	Rice	Fe	Iron ore	
		Gr	Graphite	
		Mg	Magnesium	
		Mo	Molybdenum	
		Pb	Lead	
		W	Tungsten	
		Zn	Zinc	
		⚒	Petroleum	

Mining and Energy

Most of the peninsula's mineral resources are located in North Korea. High-grade iron ore deposits are mined near the north's southwest coast. Rich deposits of anthracite coal lie near the Taedong River. Lignite coal is found in the Tumen River basin. Other important mining products in the north include magnesite, phosphate rock, tungsten, sulfur, zinc, lead, gold, silver, and copper. Coal is used to produce about 80 percent of North Korea's electric power. Hydroelectric plants supply about 12 percent. North Korea's one nuclear power plant, along with oil and natural gas, provide the rest of the country's electric power.

South Korea's most plentiful minerals are copper, iron ore, and zinc. They are in small supply, however. South Korea has to import most mining products. Many of these imports, such as coal, gold, and zinc, come from North Korea. Oil and coal are South Korea's main cooking and heating fuels. Hydroelectric plants and four nuclear power plants provide much of South Korea's electric power.

Manufacturing

About 30 percent of workers in North Korea and 20 percent of workers in South Korea work in factories making goods. The main products in both countries are cement and steel. These products are used to construct buildings and roads. The world's third-largest steel maker is Posco in South Korea. Heavy industry makes up most of North Korea's goods, such as bulldozers, diesel locomotives, engines, generators, and military equipment and weapons. Consumer goods such as food products, clothing, and shoes make up a small part of North Korea's economy.

One of Korea's main industries is cement manufacturing. This is a cement factory in South Korea.

South Korea's largest company is Hyundai, the top producer of major transportation vehicles.

In South Korea, more people work making clothing, shoes, and textiles than in any other industry. Food processing is also a major South Korean industry. South Korea is best known, however, as one of the world's biggest producers of cars, computer and computer parts, and other electronic equipment. Most of these goods are made by about thirty huge companies called *jaebol*. The largest jaebol is Hyundai, which produces most of Korea's cars, trucks, buses, and ships. Hyundai leads the world in the production of merchant ships. Other well-known jaebol are Samsung, Lucky-Goldstar (LG), and Sunkyung (SK). Samsung is the world's largest maker of memory chips. SK is South Korea's largest oil refinery. LG is known for televisions and flat-screen monitors. Cars made by Hyundai, Daewoo, and Kia make South Korea the world's sixth-largest car maker.

In 2003, Hyundai built an industrial park near Gaeseong in North Korea. About 900 South Korean textile, leather, and other manufacturing companies plan to build factories in the park. Within four years, they hope to employ about 22,000 North Koreans. This project will help both countries.

What a Won Can Buy in South Korea

Item	Price in Won	Price in U.S. $
Pair of Levi jeans	W69,000	$58.27
Pair of Nike running shoes	W55,000–199,000	$46.45–168.06
Tommy Hilfiger T-shirt	W27,000	$22.80
1.5 liters (51 ounces) Coca Cola	W1,500	$1.27
Hamburger	W1,500–3,000	$1.27–2.53
Three apples	W1,000	$0.84
Ice-cream cone	W700–1,000	$0.59–$0.84
Liter (1.057 quarts) of milk	W900–1,300	$0.76–$1.10
Hyundai Sonata	W12,760,000–13,730,000	$10,776–11,595
Liter (0.26) of gasoline	W1,300	$1.10
Harry Potter book	W10,170–12,790	$8.59–10.80
Celine Dion CD	W12,300	$10.39

Service Industries

Trade, transportation, and tourism are important service industries in both North and South Korea. North Korea has an unfavorable balance of trade, which means more money leaves the country to pay for imports than comes in to pay for exports. The main imports are coal, machinery for factories and transportation, textiles, and food grains. Goods exported include lead, magnesite, zinc, cement, and fish. North Korea's main trading partners are China, Japan, and Germany.

Since 1998, trade between the two Koreas has opened up. North Korea exports mining products to the South and imports rice. South Korea has a favorable balance of trade—it exports more than it imports. The country's largest exports are electric and electronic products, ships, cars, and chemicals. Crude oil is one of South Korea's largest imports. The United States, Japan, and China are South Korea's main trading partners.

Railroads and highways connect major cities and towns in each country. In 2000, work began to rebuild a stretch of railroad that would link Seoul, South Korea, to Jangdan, North Korea. Plans are now being made to open up a highway between the two countries. Only 6 percent of North Korea's highways are paved, which makes travel difficult. Only 262,000 cars are driven around the north. They are owned by high-ranking government and military officials. South Korea has almost three times as many miles of road as North Korea, and 77 percent of the roads are paved. About 8.8 million cars travel over these roads.

A very small percentage of North Korean roads are paved. This is North Korea's main highway.

Tourism has been important to South Korea for many years. In 2001, about 5.1 million people from other countries visited South Korea. They spent about U.S. $6.4 billion at hotels, restaurants, national parks, and museums. South Koreans also travel in their own country. They enjoy weekend breaks or longer vacations at the country's mountains, beaches, and national and provincial parks. Many tourists in South Korea stay at traditional Korean inns called *yeogwan*. The inns have ondol floors, and guests sleep on the floor on cotton-filled mattresses. North Korea is beginning to open up to tourism. In 1998, the first South Korean tourists arrived on a cruise ship tour organized by the Hyundai company. Individual tourists are limited to the city of Pyongyang. Groups of tourists are allowed to visit the Kumgang Mountains, Mount Baekdu, and the beaches at Nampo.

Tourists enjoy the culture of North Korea.

One People, One Language

THE PEOPLE OF KOREA ARE AN ETHNICALLY HOMOGENEOUS group. This means they are almost 100 percent Korean. The Korean people of today can trace their ancestry back to Mongolian people who migrated to the peninsula about 5,000 years ago. The largest groups of people from other countries are only a few thousand Chinese and Japanese. These ethnic groups make up less than 1 percent of the population in both North and South Korea.

Although South Korea has about 9,000 square miles (23,310 sq km) less land than North Korea, the South has more than twice as many people. In 2001, North Korea's population was 22,224,195; South Korea's population was 48,324,000. That means South Korea has a population density of 1,275 persons per square mile (492 persons per sq km). This is about the same population density as the state of New Jersey. North Korea's population density is 478 persons

Opposite: **The Korean people are the largest ethnic group in both North and South Korea.**

South Koreans shopping in one of their densely populated cities.

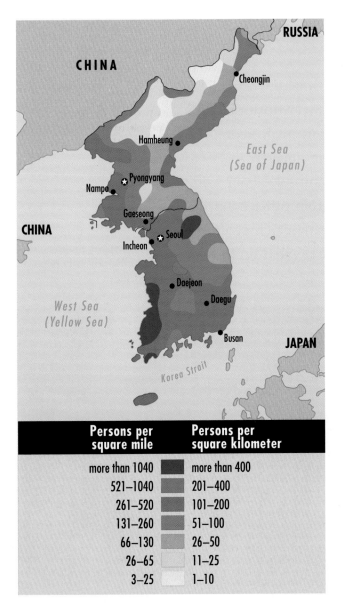

Persons per square mile		Persons per square kilometer
more than 1040		more than 400
521–1040		201–400
261–520		101–200
131–260		51–100
66–130		26–50
26–65		11–25
3–25		1–10

per square mile (185 persons per sq km), or about the population density of the state of New York.

Most Koreans in both the North and the South live in urban areas. About 81 percent of South Koreans and about 60 percent of North Koreans make their homes in cities. Most of the rest of the population live on farms or small towns along the coastal plains. Very few people live in the peninsula's mountains, which cover most of the land.

Although few people from other countries immigrate to Korea, millions of Koreans live throughout the world. Since 1903, Koreans have been immigrating to the United States. The first immigrants arrived on the U.S.-controlled Hawaiian Islands and worked on sugar and pineapple plantations. After the Korean War, many more Koreans left their war-torn land to make homes on the mainland of the United States.

Today, about 2.1 million Koreans live in U.S. cities such as New York, Chicago, and Seattle. About 640,000 Koreans live in Japan. Many of their families were moved there while Japan

occupied the peninsula. Small groups of people have escaped from North Korea and settled in China and Russia.

Residential area in Seoul

The Korean Language

Just as there is one people in Korea, there is also one written and spoken language—Korean. Spoken Korean is not related to either Chinese or Japanese. Instead, it is part of the Altaic-Turkic language group of central Asia. Although there is one

Population of Major North Korean Cities (1993 est.)		Population of Major South Korean Cities (2000 est.)	
Pyongyang (1999 est.)	3,136,000	Seoul	9,891,000
Nampo	731,448	Busan	3,664,000
Hamheung	709,000	Daegu	2,480,000
Cheongjin	582,480	Incheon	2,476,000
Gaeseong	334,433	Daejon	1,367,000

Common Korean Words and Phrases:

Annyongha-simnikka.	[AHN-nyong hah SIM-nik-gah]	Hello.
Annyeonghi gaseyo.	[AHN-nyong-hee GAH-saeh-yoh]	Good-bye.
Cheonmaneyo.	[CHON-mah-naeh-yoh]	You're welcome.
Gamsa hamnida.	[GAHM-sah HAHM-nee-dah]	Thank you.
Ye.	[YEH]	Yes.
Aniyo.	[AH-nee-yoh]	No.
Olma imnikka?	[U-mah IM-neek-gah]	How much does it cost?
Eodi iseumnigga?	[UDD-ay is-SOOM-nik-gah]	Where is . . . ?
Saram sallyeo!	[SAH-rahm SAHL-lyoh]	Help!
Sille hamnida.	[SEE-leh HAHM-nee-dah]	Excuse me.

language, there are several Korean dialects. Most Koreans can easily understand all the dialects. The Seoul dialect is the standard dialect in South Korea.

Written Korean looks quite different from English. English, French, and many other European languages are written

Street signs in hangeul

Creating an Alphabet

During the 1400s, King Sejong the Great had his scholars create an alphabet for the Korean language. Until that time, Koreans used Chinese characters to express their thoughts. The Chinese written language has thousands of characters. Instead of putting together a few characters to form many words, the Chinese had a separate character for each word or idea. Because this was a hard language to learn to write, only scholars were able to read and write. Sejong wanted more of his people to have the ability and pleasure of reading and writing.

Sejong's scholars developed the *hangeul* alphabet. In 1446, Sejong presented *hangeul* in a document called *Hunmingeongeum*, which meant "correct sounds for the instruction of the people."

At first, women and common people used *hangeul*. Scholars continued to use Chinese characters. Only after World War II did *hangeul* become the official system for writing the Korean language. Now, each October 9, South Korea celebrates Hangeul Day in honor of the adoption of the alphabet in 1446.

in Roman letters. The Korean language, however, uses the *hangeul* alphabet of ten vowels and fourteen consonants. This is a phonetic-based alphabet, so each letter has a distinct sound. In this way, letters can be put together in many

Korean Names

Korean names usually have three parts. The family name comes first, then two given or personal names. Some South Koreans still hyphenate their given names. They use a lowercase letter at the beginning of the second name, such as Chung Kyung-wha. Others use a capital letter at the beginning of each of their three names, such as Moon Sun Myung. Still others combine their two given names, such as Park Eunkyong instead of Park Eunk Yong.

A married woman does not take her husband's last name. If a woman is called Mrs. Kim, that means she is married and that her father's family name is Kim. Women are usually called names according to their relationship to their husband or children. For example, if Mrs. Kim were married to Mr. Park, she would be known as Mr. Park's wife. When Mrs. Kim becomes a mother, she would be known by the name of her oldest child.

In fact, Koreans rarely use first names when talking to one another. They usually use titles, such as Mr., Mrs., Director, Supervisor, or Principal, or they refer to one another by their station in the family, such as elder sister or younger brother.

The Hangeul Alphabet

Hangeul Vowels	English Vowels	*Hangeul* Consonants	English Consonants
ㅏ	a	ㄱ	g, k
ㅑ	ya	ㄴ	n
ㅓ	eo	ㄷ	d, t
ㅕ	yeo	ㄹ	r, l
ㅗ	o	ㅁ	m
ㅛ	yo	ㅂ	b/p
ㅜ	u	ㅅ	s
ㅠ	yu	ㅇ	ng
─	eu	ㅈ	j
ㅣ	i	ㅊ	ch
		ㅋ	k
		ㅌ	t
		ㅍ	p
		ㅎ	h

combinations to form a large vocabulary of words. In South Korea, many Chinese characters are also used in writing. However, North Koreans use only the hangeul alphabet.

At one time, some Korean vowels had accent marks, and an apostrophe was used to indicate pronunciation. In 2000, to make the language easier to write and to type, the South Korean government dropped the accents and the apostrophes. Now a *y* is added in front of vowels that had accent marks, and

an *e* replaces the apostrophe. Because there are only twenty-four characters, hangeul is an easy writing system to learn and to write. In Korean, there are no letters or sounds for the *f*, *q*, *v*, *w*, *x*, and *z* in the Roman alphabet.

Education is stressed in both Koreas. Students here study their lessons in a North Korean primary school.

Education

Education is very important in both North Korea and South Korea. The literacy rate in North Korea is about 95 percent; in South Korea it is 98 percent. In North Korea, students must attend school for eleven years, starting at age five. They study math, the Korean language, history, and science. About 8 percent of their schoolwork revolves around learning the life and ideas of Kim Il-sung and communist thought. Kim Il-sung University, founded in 1946, is the country's most important university. Difficult entrance examinations decide who will attend the school. Other students attend North Korea's more than 150 medical, technical, and agricultural universities and colleges. Education is also available to adults at night schools, correspondence schools, and classes at workplaces. The North Korean government pays for all levels of education.

In South Korea, students must attend school for nine years, from first grade through three years of middle school. A typical day for a middle-school student begins at 8:20 A.M. and ends about 4 P.M. On Saturdays, the day ends at noon. Each day includes an hour for individual study. During the week, students have a 45-minute lunch period. Subjects studied throughout the year include Korean language, English, Chinese characters, math, natural science, biology, history, sociology, ethics, home economics or industrial arts, and physical education. Each year students learn more Chinese characters.

Most students in South Korea graduate from high school and go on to college. A major college admission test is given each year. Students spend their last year in high school preparing for this test. They do not take vacations or take part in family celebrations or holidays. How well students do on this test determines which college or university they will attend. Seoul National University is the leading school. The country

has more than 120 other colleges and universities. Ewha Women's University, founded by the Methodist Church, is one of the world's largest women's schools.

Graduating university students release balloons, wishing for future employment.

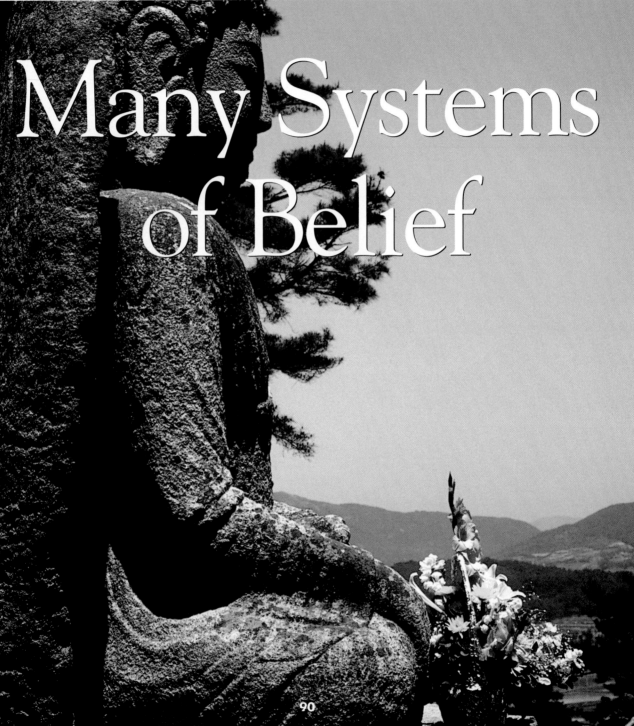

Many Systems
of Belief

Religious freedom is only truly allowed in South Korea. Here a girl prays before the Buddha Triad in Kyong-Ju, South Korea.

Although Koreans are one homogeneous people with one language, they follow many religions and belief systems. These systems include Shamanism, Buddhism, Confucianism, Daoism, and Christianity. The major systems of belief in Korea came from other countries. Buddhism arrived in Korea from India through China. Confucianism and Daoism came directly from China. At first, Christianity arrived from Europe through China. Later on, missionaries from Europe and America set up Catholic and Protestant churches on the peninsula. Korea created Cheondogyo in reaction to Western learning and religions.

The constitutions of both North and South Korea guarantee freedom of religion. South Korea's government upholds this freedom. Almost 50 percent of South Koreans say they

Opposite: **A shrine of Buddha**

Religious Followers in South Korea		Religious Followers in North Korea	
Buddhists	23%	Cheondogyoists	14%
Protestants	20%	Traditional religions	14%
Roman Catholics	7%	Buddhists	2%
Confucianists	0.5%	Christians	1%
Others: Shamanists, Muslims	0.7%	Other or no religion	69%
No religion	49%		

follow some religion. Many of them accept the beliefs of more than one religion. For example, Christians might also offer prayers at a Buddhist shrine. Buddhists take part in ancestor worship. In North Korea, however, the government controls religion. For the most part, religious worship is not allowed. Most religious practices that are not approved by the government are conducted in secret. The veneration of Kim Il-sung and Kim Jong-il has become the unofficial state religion of North Korea.

Ancient Natural Belief Systems: Shamanism and Daoism

Shamanism is Korea's oldest religion. It has been practiced since ancient times. The center of Shamanism is the shaman, or *mudang*. Today, the mudang is a woman who acts as a link between the living and the dead. Through a ceremony called *gut*, the mudang contacts spirits. During the ceremony, the mudang goes into a trance and can see the future, cast out evil spirits, and ask for good fortune from the kind spirits. *Gut* is sometimes held before a new business opens or to bring peace to a troubled family. Shamanism holds that all things have

A mudang contacts spirits in this ritual.

Korean spirit posts are thought to scare off bad or evil spirits.

spirits or souls. This includes rocks, trees, streams, and mountains. Small shaman shrines are found beneath trees or beside streams. Shaman spirit posts carved with scary faces, looking something like totem poles, still stand at the entrances of small villages. The spirit posts serve to keep evil out of the village. Today, between 2 million and 3 million South Koreans use the services of mudangs. Many mudangs fled from North Korea before and after the Korean War.

Daoism is another belief that is based on nature. *Dao*, which means "the way," is more a philosophy than a religion. The philosopher Laozi began this belief system in China in the 500s B.C. Daoism had arrived in Korea by the 100s B.C. Through Daoism, people are supposed to understand nature's laws and enter into harmony with nature. In that way, Daoists enjoy prosperity and long life. Few Koreans practice Daoism today. However, the Daoist *yang* and *eum* symbols of balance in the universe are seen throughout the country—most notably on South Korea's flag. The broken and unbroken black lines on the flag are also Daoist symbols.

Eum and yang symbols decorate doors in a South Korean village.

Confucianism

Confucianism is not a religion such as Buddhism and Christianity. There are no priests or monks, no God, no churches, and no rituals of worship. Instead, Confucianism is a system of relationships with a code of behavior. When followed, this system ensures a well-ordered society. This code of conduct was developed by Confucius (551–479 B.C.), a Chinese teacher and philosopher. According to Confucius, there were five ranks of superior/subordinate relationships: ruler/subject or government/citizen, father/son, older person/younger person, husband/wife, and friend/friend. In each relationship, the weaker/younger person submits to the stronger/older one, but the stronger person is obliged to protect the weaker one. Only in the friend relationship is there equality, and that is only if the two persons are the same age and gender. Respect for one's elders led to respect for ancestors. Thus, Confucianism also called for special ceremonies of ancestor worship. In addition, Confucianism required that government officials be scholars who had passed a rigorous civil-service examination. To prepare for this test, young men spent years studying in Confucian academies.

Historians believe that Confucianism was in Korea before A.D. 100. Later, it became the official philosophy or state religion of the Joseon Dynasty

Chinese teacher and philosopher Confucius

(1392–1910). Koreans followed Confucianism so strictly that Chinese visitors said that Korea was more Confucian than China. Today, Koreans still practice the ideas of Confucius. They respect their parents, honor their ancestors, maintain strong ties to their families, are loyal to their company or school, and make lifelong friends. The leaders in North Korea have used Confucian traditions to keep the people loyal to them and to their government. Through Confucianism, Koreans have a strong sense of community. When something bad happens, such as the economic crisis in 1997, everyone works together with the government to pull Korea out of trouble. The Confucian attitude toward studying has carried over to regular schools and colleges. In addition, some families send their sons to after-school Confucian academies to become Confucian scholars.

Today, there are more than 200 Confucian academies in Korea. Each academy has a library, a lecture hall, sleeping rooms, a shrine, and a pavilion. Twice a year, ceremonies are held at the academies to honor Confucius and Korean

Confucian ritual at the Jongmyo Shrine

Confucian scholars. In the spring, government officials put on colorful Confucian ceremonial robes at the Jongmyo Shrine in Seoul to honor the Joseon kings. In September, the colorful Seokjeonje ceremony honors Confucius's birthday at Korea's main Confucian shrine. This takes place with music, dance, and offerings of food at the Daeseongjon Shrine at Seonggyungwan University in Seoul.

Buddhism

Buddhism was founded in India by Prince Siddhartha Gautama about 528 B.C. Later, Siddhartha became known as Buddha, "The Enlightened One." Enlightenment is the goal of all Buddhists. Enlightenment is achieved when a person eliminates all desire because desire is the cause of all suffering. Until people attain enlightenment, they must go through a cycle of birth, death, and rebirth known as reincarnation. Besides Buddha, there are many gods and goddesses in the Buddhist religion.

Buddhism entered Korea from China in the A.D. 300s. It became the state religion in each of the Three Kingdoms, in Unified Silla, and of the Koryo Dynasty. In the mid-1900s, Buddhism was considered old-fashioned.

This painting of Buddha can be found in the Temple of Yungju in South Korea.

The *Tripitaka Koreana* represents more than 81,000 wooden print blocks of Buddhist teachings.

By the 1970s, Koreans had become interested in Buddhism again. Many Buddhist temples were rebuilt, and a Buddhist Bible was published. Today, Buddhism has the largest following of all of Korea's religions. In South Korea, there are more than 11,000 temples and more than 26,000 monks and nuns. These religious people work for social reform and carry out charitable activities. Temples can be found off busy city streets or in forested mountain locales. Two of the most famous Buddhist temples in South Korea are Bulguksa and Haeinsa. The Haeinsa Temple is the storage place for the famous *Tripitaka Koreana*. This consists of 81,340 wooden printing blocks that contain the world's most complete set of Buddhist teachings. More than 52 million Chinese characters were carved into the blocks. In North Korea, the government took over the Buddhist temples and now uses them for nonreligious purposes.

In recent years, the government has allowed the establishment of a Buddhist academy and services in a few temples.

Christianity: Catholics and Protestants

Like Buddhism, Christianity first reached Korea through China. This religion teaches that Jesus Christ is the son of God and that he died on a cross to redeem the sins of all people. During the 1600s, Catholic writings were carried in by officials of the Joseon Dynasty. In 1784, the first priests arrived.

The Bulguksa Temple

Beginning in A.D. 751, for a period of more than twenty years, Korean artisans built the massive complex known as the Bulguksa Temple. *Bulguk* means "Land of Buddha." The temple complex is located below the foothills of Mount Tohamsan near the ancient city of Gyeongju. It represents the height of Korea's Buddhist culture and art. In the courtyard stand two of Korea's most beautiful stone pagodas. The simplicity of the Seokgatap Pagoda symbolizes the spiritual way to enlightenment. The more decorative Dabotap Pagoda represents the desires and complexities of the world. Bulguksa also has two large seated, bronze statues of Buddha.

The government did not approve of Catholicism because Catholicism did not allow ancestor worship. In the early 1800s, thousands of Catholics were executed. In the late 1800s, after Korea had opened to trade with other countries, Protestant missionaries from England and the United States arrived. Catholic and Protestant missionaries established schools, universities, hospitals, and orphanages. During the Japanese Occupation, Christian missionaries worked with Koreans to win back Korea's independence. At that time, Pyongyang had a large Christian population. After North Korea was established, however, Christians fled south to avoid persecution and execution.

Today, Christianity is the second-largest religion in Korea. It includes Catholicism and the following Protestant denominations: Methodists, Presbyterians, Anglicans, Latter-day Saints (Mormons), and several evangelical, gospel churches. In the North, a small number of Christians are allowed to worship under government supervision. Others practice their religion in underground services. In recent years, South Korean Christians have been outspoken supporters of democracy and human rights in their country. South Korea has about

A Visit by the Pope

Pope John Paul II visited Seoul in 1984 to celebrate the 200th anniversary of Catholicism in Korea. At that time, he canonized 93 Korean martyrs who had died for their faith during persecutions in the 1800s. This gave Korea the world's fourth-largest number of Catholic saints. Before 1984, the canonization ceremony had never been held outside the Vatican—the pope's home near Rome, Italy.

Worshipers crowd the Youido Full Gospel Church.

60,000 Protestant churches and more than 1,000 Catholic churches. There are about 5,000 Christian churches in Seoul. The Youido Full Gospel Church in Seoul is one of the world's largest churches. Its message that Christ brings health, prosperity, and salvation appeals to more than 700,00 South Koreans. South Korea's most prominent Catholic church is the Myeongdong Cathedral in Seoul. The Gothic-style building was completed in 1898 on the site of Korea's first Catholic church, which was built in 1784.

Cheondogyo

In the 1860s, Choeo Jeu began the Donghak Movement, or Eastern Learning Movement. This was a reaction to the Western learning that was spreading through Korea by the Catholic Church. Although Choeo was executed by the government in 1864, his movement gained many followers. They changed the movement's name to Cheondogyo, "Teachings of the Heavenly Way." The main beliefs of Cheondogyo are that all people are equal and that there is divinity or God in each person.

Today, about 1 million South Koreans are followers of Cheondogyo. It is the largest religion in North Korea, with about 3 million believers. The government has allowed this religion to grow because it is an original Korean religion. Also, some of its beliefs, such as equality, help support government propaganda. In addition, this religion has organized a political party.

Strong Cultural Traditions

KOREANS TREASURE THEIR RICH CULTURAL TRADITIONS in the arts and sports. This is especially true in North Korea, where the Kim regimes have promoted the idea that Korea and Koreans are superior to other countries and other people. North Koreans point to traditional Korean arts, crafts, and sports to support this idea. The South Korean government has designated several buildings and art objects, such as pagodas, vases, and wood printing blocks, as National Treasures. Traditional crafts, games, and musical and dance performances are honored as Intangible Cultural Properties. Specially skilled people who perform these arts and crafts are named as Human Cultural Treasures. The governments of both North Korea and South Korea have ministries that regulate and promote culture and sports.

Opposite: **Members of Little Angel, a Korean children's dance group, perform while in traditional dress.**

Traditional Crafts

Korea's traditional craft work is recognized throughout the world for its beauty and delicacy. Throughout the centuries, Korean artists and craftspeople have worked with paper, wood, cloth, and ceramics to create beautiful objects for everyday use. Geometric patterns of blue, green, red, blue, and browns decorate much Korean craft work. Symbols from nature, such as the sun and moon, cranes, fish, butterflies, trees, and streams are also common.

Celedon pottery on display

Celadon is Korea's most famous pottery, with its bluish-green glazes and inlaid designs of clouds and cranes. Artists make cups, bowls, pitchers, vases, and other dishes with celadon. Korean potters continue to use traditional techniques and designs. In fact, traditional kilns have been rebuilt in the countryside so that potters can re-create high-quality pottery today. Many traditional celadon pieces are found in museums outside Korea.

Korean crafters also show their creativity with silk, hemp, ramie, and cotton cloth. *Bojagi* are colorful square wrapping cloths. Small pieces of leftover material are sewn together in geometric patchwork designs to make the bojagi squares. Long ago, Koreans believed that keeping things wrapped up brought good fortune. These square cloths come in various sizes and can be folded for use as money belts, backpacks, tablecloths, or laundry sacks. Some bojagi look like an envelope or pouch and have ties attached. Items can be safely wrapped up in them and put away. Special bojagi used for weddings and other

A bojagi, or wrapping cloth, embroidered with flowers

Korean Weddings

In the past, a Korean wedding began with the bride being carried in a special wedding box to the groom's parents' home. During the ceremonies, the couple wore special wedding hanbok, traditional Korean clothing. Today, weddings take place in churches or huge wedding halls. In both North and South Korea, the bride usually wears a white Western-style wedding gown, and the groom wears a dark suit. After the ceremony, the couple put on hanbok and go to the groom's parents' home. There, they honor their parents with low bows and take part in a special tea ceremony. The bride's parents are expected to provide them with three keys: the keys to a car, an apartment, and an office if the groom is a lawyer or doctor.

ceremonies are embroidered with designs of flowers and birds. Korean embroidery is called *jasu*. Besides decorating bojagi, jasu is found on *hanbok*, pillow cases, eyeglass cases, and purses. At one time, only nobles and royalty could wear or own clothing or cloth with jasu.

Colorful paper lanterns hang at the Bulguksa Temple to celebrate the Buddha's birthday.

Korea is also famous for its paper crafts. In rural areas, mulberry bark paper is still used for windows and interior sliding doors. Decorative jars, bowls, baskets, trays, stationery cases, and jewelry boxes are a few items that crafters still make from paper. They paste many layers of paper together for strength. Items that must withstand pressure, such as writing trays, are reinforced with wooden rods. Colorful designs are painted on the paper, which is then varnished with a mixture of persimmon juice, rice glue, and oil. The most popular paper goods made today are lanterns displayed on Buddha's birthday, fans, and kites.

Art

Early Korean art is divided into paintings for the noble class and folk painting. Paintings for the noble class focused on flowers, birds, and landscapes with trees, water, and stones.

Artists used restrained brushwork and neutral colors. Rarely were people shown in these paintings. Folk paintings also contained objects from nature but presented them with humor. Brushwork in folk paintings was lively, and artists used bright colors. The tiger was a favorite object in Korean folk paintings. The animals were often shown as friendly, funny, and even stupid. Korean artists also did paintings with religious themes showing Buddhist gods and people observing the Confucian ideals of loyalty and respect. Many early Korean sculptures were shaped like Buddhist deities. The most famous ones are at the Seokguram Grotto. Thirty-nine figures of Buddhist gods are chiseled in the wall. They surround an 11.5 foot (3.5-m) seated statue of Buddha.

Modern Korean artists are using the spirit of traditional art in their works. For example, Sanjong uses black ink in a controlled stroke, but his paintings express a modern sense of freedom. Other artists are doing public art on walls of schools,

Paintings that included objects from nature were painted for Korea's noble class.

Kim Hong-do: Artist of the People

Kim Hong-do (1745–1806) was a government artist during the Joseon Dynasty. He is considered to be one of the three great masters of that dynasty. Kim is known for his portraits of royalty and his landscapes created from real scenes as he traveled around the country. However, he is best known for his scenes of everyday people at work and at play, such as *ssireum* wrestlers and village musicians and dancers. These paintings left a historical record of the lives of common people. Kim died a lonely and poor man. Today, his works are designated as National Treasures and can be seen in Korea's art museums.

UNESCO World Cultural Heritage List

In 2003, South Korea had ten sites on UNESCO's list of 754 important places for the world's cultural heritage. The United States, which is almost 100 times larger than South Korea, has eighteen sites. The sites for South Korea, and the year they were added to the list, are given below.

1995: Seokguram Grotto and Bulguksa Temple, Gyeongsangbuk Province

1995: The Tripitaka Koreana woodblocks and their repository at the Janggneong Panjeon at the Haeinsa Temple, Gyeongsangnam Province

1995: Jongmyo Shrine, Seoul

1997: Changdeokgung Palace Complex, Seoul, and Hwaseong Fortress, Suwon

2000: Dolmen Sites at Gochang, Hwasun, and Ganghwa

2000: Gyeongju Historic Areas, the entire city of Gyeongju

hospitals, and subway stations. Korea's most popular modern artist is the sculptor Paik Namjune (1932–present). His unusual work consists of objects such as television sets, speakers, and musical instruments. He tries to get people to examine what they really see and hear on television. *V-ramid*, a pyramid with masks and tele-vision screens, and *Man on Horseback*, with a man made of television sets, are two of Paik's well-known pieces.

Performing Arts: Music, Dance, and Film

Koreans enjoy traditional, classical, and popular music. The most famous traditional Korean song is the *pansori*, which the South Korean government has designated as an Important Intangible Cultural Property. Pansori are long, dramatic songs

A woman performs a traditional Korean song, the pansori.

performed by one woman, accompanied by a performer on a *buk* (barrel drum). Only six pansori songs remain in existence.

Groups of singers often use the *gayageum*, a 12-stringed zither, when accompanying themselves. Other stringed instruments include the *ajaeng*, a 7-stringed zither, and the *haegeum*, a 2-stringed fiddle. Besides the buk, other Korean percussion instruments include the *kkwaenggwari* (small gong), *jing* (large gong), and *janggu* (hourglass drum). Drums and gongs are played by dancers in many folk dances, as well as by drum and gong ensembles. Korean wind instruments are played in small groups with other instruments. The main wind instruments are the *daegeum* (large bamboo transverse flute), *hojeok* (conical oboe), *piri* (bamboo oboe), and *tungso* (bamboo vertical flute).

Drummers ensemble perform on the janggu.

Traditional Korean dances include folk, court, and religious performances. *Pulgmulnori* is a popular farmer's dance. The dancers' hats have long streamers that they swirl in wide loops as they dance and beat out the rhythm with drums and gongs. In masked dramas, another popular folk dance, performers wear large full-head masks with

Folk dancers perform a mask dance.

exaggerated expressions. In the past, the dancers wore masks to hide their identity so they would not be caught making fun of the ruling class. Today, the dances are performed as entertainment in several villages. *Taepyeongmu* ("Dance of Great Peace") is a court dance from the Joseon Kingdom. It was performed as a prayer for national peace and prosperity. In *Seungmu*, the monk dance or Buddhist dance, the dancers move in harmony with their surroundings and put the audience in a dreamlike state. All three of these dances are classified as Important Intangible Cultural Properties.

Modern classical music is also popular in Korea. Several Koreans have become known worldwide as classical composers, singers, and instrumentalists. Yun Isang (1917–1995) wrote more than 150 works, including symphonies and operas with political themes. Ahn Eaktay (1905–1965) wrote Korea's national anthem. He also crafted *Korea Fantasia*, a long piece that expresses the highs and lows of Korea's 5,000-year history. Jo Su-mi (1962–present) is Korea's most famous opera star. She has sung in major opera houses around the world and was named Best Soprano of the Year in 1993 by Italian opera critics. The Chung Trio is perhaps South Korea's best-known group of classical musicians. Chung Myung-hwa (1944–present) plays the cello. Her sister Chung Kyung-wha (1944–present) is an accomplished violinist. Their brother Chung Myung-whun (1953–present) is an award-winning pianist and conductor.

Koreans have been making films since the 1919 production of *Righteous Revenge*. Between the 1920s and 1980, Korea's film industry was quite unsteady. Since 1980, the industry has moved forward with several award-winning films. The 1993 film *Seopeyeonje* ("The Western Style") tells the story of a family of pansori singers and the problems they have in the modern world. The 1999 spy-thriller *Shiri* was a hit at the box office. In 2000, *Chunhyangjeon*, the story of a young woman's loyalty to her husband, was the first Korean film to be entered in the Cannes Film Festival. South Korea now has its own film festivals each in year in Busan, Bucheon, and Jeonju.

Literature

Korea's earliest literature was written in Chinese characters. Histories were some of the first prose written. During the Goryeo Dynasty, two accounts of the Three Kingdoms Period were *Samguk Sagi* and *Samguk Yusa*. The most important history of the Joseon Dynasty is the *Joseon Wangjo Sillok*. This history included an encyclopedia with sections on agriculture, the economy, music, geography, and many other subjects.

Koreans have enjoyed many forms of poetry. The most long-lasting style is known as *sijo*. This form of poetry has three lines with about fifteen syllables per line. Sijo are personal poems about feelings such as love, grief, or anger. Some sijo, however, has political or satirical themes. Women write many love sijo, while men write political sijo.

After the hangeul alphabet was invented, some Korean writers began using it instead of Chinese characters. Heo Kyun (1569–1618) wrote *The Story of Hong Kiltong*, the first novel in hangeul. In the novel, Hong Kiltong sets up a classless society on an island without nobles and their laws. Noblewomen in the Korean court also wrote novels in hangeul. The most famous of these novels is *The Memoirs of Lady Hyegyeong*, written by Princess Hyegyeong (1735–1815). This work tells the true story of how her father-in-law, the king, killed her husband.

Since the 1900s, Korean writers have been influenced by Western ideas. The poet Kim Soweol used ordinary speech and slang in his poems. Seo Cheongju's anthology *Unforgettable Things* has poems that describe the many changes Koreans have undergone since the 1950s. One of South Korea's best-known novelists is Ahn Cheong-hyo. He wrote his novels in both English and Korean. Modern literature in North Korea is heavily censored. There, most stories revolve around heroes from Korea's history or glorify more current heroes who have fought for North Korea, especially the leader Kims.

Traditional and Modern Sports

Korea has a long history of sports and recreation. The most famous sport to begin in Korea is *taegwondo*, use of fists and feet to disable an opponent. Koreans trace this martial art to the beginning of their civilization. At one time, taegwondo was part of Korea's national defense system. Before becoming a soldier, Korean men had to be skilled in taegwondo. Today it is a sport used to discipline the mind, body, and spirit. People all over the world practice taegwondo. It became an official game of the Olympics in 2000.

Taegwondo has been a part of Korean life for centuries. Here, junior high school students compete in a tournament.

Ssireum, or Korean wrestling, is another sport that began in Korea. It can be traced back to about 37 B.C. Ssireum started as a competition among villagers before becoming a martial art. Today, ssireum is a sport with televised matches performed in stadiums. Two wrestlers grab each other's cloth sash and try to push each other out of an encircled sand ring. Another traditional sport is archery using a bow

Two wrestlers compete in an age-old ssireum match during the May Festival.

The Seoul Olympics and Koreans in Other Olympics

In 1988, the twenty-fourth Summer Olympic Games were held in Seoul, South Korea. Peace, Harmony, and Progress was the theme of the games, in which more than 13,000 athletes from 160 countries took part. For these games, South Korea built the Seoul Sports Complex, which includes the Olympic Stadium, two gymnasiums, an indoor swimming pool, and a baseball stadium. Other sports facilities and training areas were built in Seoul, as well as in Busan. South Korea's athletes placed fourth in the overall medal count.

Koreans have taken part in Olympics all over the world. In the 1936 Berlin Olympics, Sohn Kee-jeong won the gold for the marathon. He was part of Japan's team because Korea was under Japanese rule at that time. At the 1992 Barcelona games, Hwang Young-jo won the gold in the marathon for South Korea. Many other South Koreans have won gold medals. The most recent winners were on the women's speed-skating team in the 2002 Winter Games in Salt Lake City, Utah.

Since 1948, the two Koreas have sent separate teams to the Olympic Games. However, in the 2000 Summer Games in Sydney, Australia, the two teams marched together for the first time in the opening ceremonies.

Jeonju World Cup Stadium

The Jeonju World Cup Stadium was built for the 2002 FIFA Men's World Cup Games in soccer. The stadium's seating areas and roof look like the traditional paper folding fan made in Jeonju. The columns and cables that hold up the roof look like the 12-stringed *gayageum*, a traditional musical instrument. The 2002 games were played in both Korea and Japan. This was the first time that two countries hosted the World Cup. South Korea competed in the World Cup and placed fourth.

with ends that curve away from the shooter. Many South Korean women have become skilled at this sport and have won gold medals at Olympics and other world championship games.

Soccer is a modern sport that has gained popularity in Korea. Children play soccer in their neighborhoods and schools. Both North and South Korea have professional men's and women's soccer teams. North Korea's women's team won a gold medal at the 2003 Universiade held in Daegu, South Korea. Also in 2003, North Korea's and South Korea's women's national teams made it to the women's World Cup, held in the United States. Both Korean teams were eliminated during the first round. South Korea's men's national soccer team has a huge following. Their fans are called Red Devils because they wear red shirts and caps.

Professional baseball and golf have a following in South Korea. Several professional Korean baseball players have become known worldwide. Park Chan-ho and Kim Byung-hyun have been pitchers on U.S. Major League teams, and Choi Hee-sup is a promising first baseman. In the world of golf, Choi Kyung-ju won three major men's world titles in 2002 and 2003. Female golfer Pak Se-ri won four important women's championships in 1998 and was chosen Ladies' Rookie of the Year. At age twenty, she was the youngest woman to gain that distinction.

The governments of both Koreas encourage their citizens to take part in sports. In recent years, more Koreans include sports as leisure activities alone, with their families, or as part of a company team. Tennis, bicycling, jogging, swimming, and hiking are a few of the more popular sports. In 1977, Ko Sang-don successfully climbed to the top of Mount Everest in Tibet. Since then, more Koreans have become interested in climbing the many mountains of Korea.

Pak Se-ri is South Korea's leading female golfer.

Daily Life and Special Occasions

K OREAN MEN AND WOMEN WORK LONG HOURS ON FARMS and in factories, offices, and the home. Korean children study hard in school and after school. However, they also find time to get together with family and friends. Eating traditional Korean foods is an important part of most gatherings. Although most Koreans live in modern apartment buildings or in newer rural houses, traditional elements of style are still found in most homes. In addition, Koreans wear traditional clothing for many special family occasions and national festivals.

Opposite: **A vendor sells various herbs to his customers.**

Korean Families

The family holds a special place in the life of Koreans. Three of the five Confucian relationships deal with respect within the family: children for parents, wives for husbands, and juniors for elders. Children are treasured by their parents and grandparents. As they grow up, children treat their parents and grandparents with respect and take care of them in their old age. Younger brothers and sisters respect their older brothers and

A family shares a meal in the traditional style.

sisters. In fact, they do not even call them by name. Instead, they call them *eonni* (elder sister) or *oppa* (elder brother).

In the past, a Korean household was made up of three generations. This included grandparents, parents, children, and even aunts and uncles. Today, most Korean households have only two generations: parents and their children. Because North Korea has a population shortage, couples are encouraged to have large families. In highly populated South Korea, most couples limit themselves to two children. Although couples still hope to have at least one son, families that only have daughters are becoming more acceptable. In South Korea, daughters now share equally with sons in inheritance rights. For hundreds of years, only sons—and sometimes only the eldest son—could inherit family property.

Because both mothers and fathers work outside the home in North Korea, children are taken care of in nurseries and daycare centers. In South Korea, few mothers work outside the home. They are called the "inside person" because their job is to raise their children and to take care of the household. South Korean mothers spend many hours helping their children with schoolwork and taking them to after-school classes in English and math. South Korean fathers usually leave early in the morning for work. They are called "the outside person." Many evenings they return home after the family has had dinner.

Korean families try to make the most of their time together. They go on bike rides through parks, take trips to national or provincial parks, and fish in nearby rivers and streams. They also keep in close contact with other family members, such as grandparents and aunts and uncles. Important family occasions include weddings, birthdays, and New Year's festivals.

Special Occasions: Three Birthdays

Koreans use a method different from North Americans to count a person's age. When a baby is born, Koreans say he or she is in the first year or "one." On Lunar New Year's Day, all Koreans gain a year, so the child is in his or her second year, or "two." Modern Korean families also celebrate birthdays on the actual birth date with parties, gifts, and their own version of the song "Happy Birthday."

In the past, many children died before the 100th day of life. A ceremony called *baegil* was held for those who lived 100 days. It was believed that they were healthy enough to reach adulthood. At baegil, the baby was given its name. Baegil is still performed today. Family and friends offer thanks to the "grandmother spirit" who is believed to watch over infants. Then they share a feast of wonderful foods.

On the first anniversary of a child's birth, the birthday celebration called *dol* is observed. The child is dressed in a hanbok and placed behind a low table filled with tall stacks of fruits and rice cakes. Several other items are placed in front of the child. Whichever item the child picks up first is supposed to predict his future. Money means a career in business, while a piece of cake might lead to government service. A length of string points to a long life. The choice of a pencil means the child could become a scholar, and a musical instrument predicts a possible musician or artist.

A Korean's sixtieth birthday, called *hwangap*, has been important for two reasons. In the past, not many people lived to be 60 years old. Also, the lunar calendar used by Koreans is based on a 60-year cycle. Each year has a different name. By living through the cycle, a person returns to the year of his or her birth. Family and friends honor the 60-year-old with deep bows, gifts, and feasting on special foods. Today, many 60-year-old Koreans observe their hwangap by taking a vacation.

Korean Meals

Various dishes are prepared for this family's meal.

Korean foods are known for their great variety, strong flavors, and hot spices. Slightly sticky, white rice balances these flavors at every meal. In South Korea, people eat three meals a day. Because of the food shortage in North Korea, many people there eat only one or two meals a day. Rice is in short supply, so North Koreans substitute foods made of cornmeal or wheat for their main dish.

In South Korea, rice and *gimchi* are part of every meal. A typical breakfast consists of soup, vegetables, meat or fish, rice, and gimchi. Lunch might be a salad, corn, meat, rice, and gimchi. Dinner could include beef and crab, beans, other vegetables, rice, and gimchi. Cold drinks such as fruit juices or punch are served before meals. Tea and a dessert of fruit or sweet rice cakes are served after dinner.

Korean meals are served on a low table with everyone sitting on the floor. Each person has his or her own bowls of rice and soup. Several bowls with side dishes of vegetables, meat, and fish are arranged in the center of the table, along with bowls of gimchi and soy sauces. Everyone takes the side dishes from these bowls with their chopsticks. They then might dip the food into a bowl of soy sauce or pick up some gimchi for seasoning.

Gimchi: **Korea's National Dish**

The first written description of making *gimchi* dates to about A.D. 1250. Gimchi is served every day at every meal. Basically, gimchi is fermented or pickled vegetables, such as Chinese cabbage, cucumbers, or radish roots, seasoned with red peppers. Onions, carrots, seaweed, garlic, and pine nuts are other ingredients. There are about 170 varieties of gimchi. Two or three kinds are served with meals. Gimchi is also used as a fiery seasoning in soups and stews. In the past, families made large crocks of gimchi that they stored outdoors during the winter. Today, some families still make their own, but gimchi is available in supermarkets throughout Korea. Because gimchi is low in calories and cholesterol and high in fiber, it is promoted as a health food. Because gimchi has more vitamins than apples, Koreans say, "Gimchi each day keeps the doctor away."

Bulgogi: An Easy-to-Make Special Occasion Food

Bulgogi, like gimchi, is another food closely linked to Korea. Unlike gimchi, bulgogi is not served every day. Bulgogi is party food. Its name means "fired meat" or "barbecue." Like most barbecue food, bulgogi is easy to make, as shown in the following recipe.

Ingredients

1 pound beef sirloin
$\frac{1}{4}$ cup soy sauce
1 teaspoon honey
1 tablespoon sugar
2 cloves minced garlic
$\frac{1}{4}$ chopped onion
$\frac{1}{2}$ teaspoon sesame oil
$\frac{1}{8}$ teaspoon ground black pepper
Lettuce
Slices of green pepper

Instructions: Cut meat across the grain into thin slices. Tenderize each slice by tapping with the dull side of a knife. In a bowl, mix the next seven ingredients. Place meat in the mixture. Cover the bowl and set it in the refrigerator for an hour. Preheat the broiler of the oven or have someone fire up a barbecue grill. On high heat, cook the meat slices about 2 minutes on each side. Wrap the cooked meat with green pepper slices and place on lettuce leaves. Asparagus and mushrooms are sometimes served with bulgogi.

Housing

Many changes have taken place in housing since the 1950s. Koreans have maintained some traditional elements, however. In the past, Koreans in urban and rural areas lived in houses made with wood beams, clay walls, and thatch roofs. The homes of wealthy persons had tile roofs. Rooms were separated by sliding doors made of mulberry paper. The most remarkable part of traditional housing was the heating system, called *ondol*. Channels under the floor carried hot air from the kitchen fire to other rooms in the house. Because the floors were warm, people sat on the floor to eat and at night pulled out mats to sleep on the floor.

Two types of single-family homes sit side by side on Jeju Island.

Today, single-family homes are made of concrete with tiled roofs. These homes are located mainly in rural villages and suburbs of Korea's cities and can cost between $211,000 in Seoul and about $591,000 outside Seoul. However, most Koreans throughout the peninsula live in large apartment/ condominium buildings. This includes people in rural areas of North Korea. The price of a condominium can range from $194,000 at the end of the subway line outside of Seoul to $380,000 within the city.

The ondol heating system is still in use in Korea. The pipes under the floors now carry heated water. Electric coils under the floors provide heat in apartment buildings. In the summer, air conditioning is provided through the ondol system. Almost all Korean homes have electricity and hot water. In Seoul, a month's electric bill can range from $30 to $68; water might cost $42 a month. Most Koreans still sleep on the floor and sit on the floor to eat. However, some homes have Western-style beds and tables and chairs.

The *Hanbok*

Koreans wear Western-style clothing to work and to school and most of the time around the house. However, traditional clothing called *hanbok* is worn on holidays and special family occasions. Parts of this costume date back to the A.D. 600s. The women's hanbok has a long, full, wrap-around skirt (*chima*) and a short jacket or blouse (*jeogori*) tied with a bow to one side. The men's hanbok has a short jacket (*jeogori*) and baggy pants (*baji*) that tie at the ankles. Men and women wear a long, full coat (*durumagi*) over their outfits. Hanbok for both men and women can be all white. They also come in vivid colors. Both men and women wear colorful shoes with turned-up toes as part of the hanbok. Because the hanbok has no pockets, both men and women carry drawstring purses (*jumeoni*). Hanbok are also made for boys, girls, and infants. Because the hanbok is such graceful and comfortable clothing, Korean fashion designers are making modern styles of hanbok. Some Koreans are beginning to wear these new styles every day.

Korean Holidays and Festivals

Between national holidays and traditional festivals, Koreans have something to celebrate every month. Each province or city has its own festivals, such as the World Festival for Island Cultures held in Jeju Island Province. Other festivals celebrate nature, such as the Cherry Blossom Festival held in the city of Jinhae in early spring. Still other festivals honor local products, such as the Ginseng Festival in the city of Geumsan in September. The two most important Korean holidays are *Seollal* and *Chuseok*.

Fan dancers perform at the Shilla Cultural Festival

Seollal, or Lunar New Year, is the first big celebration of the year. This holiday lasts for several days at the end of January or beginning of February. Koreans return to their hometowns or to their oldest relative's home. On the first day of the New Year, Koreans wear hanbok. The first thing in the morning on Seollal, Korean families offer their deceased ancestors special foods in a ceremony called *charye*. Later, young members of the family perform *sebae*, a special low bow to their parents, grandparents, and other elders. The bow expresses wishes for happiness and good health in the coming year. In return, the elders give the children pouches of money called *sebae-don*. Then they eat *tteokguk*, a soup with sliced rice cakes, meat, and vegetables. With this soup, Koreans acknowledge that they are one year older. On Seollal, rather than on their birthday, Koreans grow one year older. After eating, Korean children and adults play traditional games. Boys spin tops in a game called *paengi-chigi*. Kite flying is also popular. Koreans believe their kites will take away bad luck and bring good luck for the new year. Today, fewer Koreans play these traditional games. Many now turn to television or to video and computer games.

Neolttwigi: Korean Seesaw

Neolttwigi is played by three girls wearing hanboks on Seollal. A wide board is centered over a rolled-up straw mat. One girl sits on the middle of the board. Two other girls stand on each end of the board. The first girl jumps up and lands on her end of the board, which in turn sends the other girl into the air. When the second girl lands, the first girl is again sent up. At one time, this was the only time of the year when girls had a chance to look over the courtyard wall and see the outside world.

During their other major holiday, Chuseok, Koreans give thanks for the good harvest in the fall. The night before Chuseok under the Harvest Moon, ten to twenty women in hanbok perform a circle dance called *ganggangsullae*. Also on that night, Korean families make *songpyeon*, crescent-shaped rice cakes filled with sesame seeds, chestnut paste, or beans. In the morning, they visit their ancestors' graves. At the graves they perfom low bows, make offerings of the songpyeon, and clean the area around the grave. Later in the day, they tell stories about their ancestors. Some play traditional games and sports, such as turtle tag (*geobuknori*), archery, and wrestling (ssireum).

Seollal and Chuseok are no longer officially celebrated in North Korea. The major holidays in North Korea revolve around important events in the country's history, such as Liberation Day on August 15, Independence Day on September 9, and the birthdays of Kim Il-sung and Kim Jong-il.

These events are marked with large parades and rallies in the stadium in Pyongyang. South Korea also celebrates Liberation Day with parades and speeches that recall the end of Japanese rule over Korea on August 15, 1945. With both countries working toward reunification or reconciliation, perhaps all of the Korean people will be able to celebrate Liberation Day together sometime in the future.

National Holidays in North Korea (NK) and South Korea (SK)

Holiday	Date
New Year's Day (NK, SK)	January 1
Seollal (Lunar New Year) (SK)	January or February
Kim Jong-il's Birthday (NK)	February 16
Independence Movement Day (SK)	March 1
Arbor Day (SK)	April 5
Kim Il-sung's Birthday (NK)	April 15
Foundation of the People's Army (NK)	April 25
Buddha's Birthday (SK)	April or May
International Worker's Day (NK)	May 1
Children's Day (SK)	May 5
Memorial Day (SK)	June 6
Constitution Day (SK)	July 17
Victory Day (NK)	July 27
Liberation Day (NK, SK)	August 15
Independence Day (NK)	September 9
Chuseok (Thanksgiving/Harvest Festival) (SK)	September or October
National Foundation Day (NK,SK)	October 3
Hangeul–National Alphabet Day (SK)	October 9
Foundation of the Korean Workers' Party (NK)	October 10
Christmas (SK)	December 25
Constitution Day (NK)	December 27

Timeline

Korean History

Japan forces Korea open to trade.	1876
The United States forces Korea to trade.	1882
Japan annexes Korea as a colony.	1910
The March First Movement stages protests for independence.	1919
Koreans are forced to serve in the Japanese military and as laborers in Japan's war effort.	1930s–1945
Korea is divided after Japan surrenders in World War II.	1945
The U.S. occupies South Korea and the USSR occupies North Korea.	1945–1948
In August, the Republic of Korea is formed in the south; in September, the Democratic People's Republic of Korea is formed in the north.	1948
The Korean War is fought, ending with a cease-fire and a still divided Korean Peninsula.	1950–1953
South Korea becomes known as the "Miracle on the Han" for its booming economy.	1970s
The first free and democratic elections in South Korea take place.	1987
South Korea begins trade and diplomatic relations with China and Russia.	Early 1990s
Kim Il-sung, leader of North Korea, dies.	1994
Kim Jong-il becomes leader of North Korea; South Korea experiences an economic crisis.	1997
In June, the leaders of North and South Korea meet for the first time in Pyongyang; President Kim Dae-jung is awarded the Nobel Peace Prize.	2000
North Korea announces that it is making nuclear weapons.	2003
President Roh Moo-hyun is impeached and then reinstated.	2004

World History

1914	World War I breaks out.
1917	The Bolshevik Revolution brings communism to Russia.
1929	Worldwide economic depression begins.
1939	World War II begins, following the German invasion of Poland.
1945	World War II ends.
1957	The Vietnam War starts.
1969	Humans land on the moon.
1975	The Vietnam War ends.
1979	Soviet Union invades Afghanistan.
1983	Drought and famine begin in Africa.
1989	The Berlin Wall is torn down, as communism crumbles in Eastern Europe.
1991	Soviet Union breaks into separate states.
1992	Bill Clinton is elected U.S. president.
2000	George W. Bush is elected U.S. president.
2001	Terrorists attack World Trade Towers, New York, and the Pentagon, Washington, D.C.

Fast Facts

*For most items, there are two sets of facts—one for North Korea (NK) and one for South Korea (SK). If the fact is the same for both countries, only one fact is given.

Official names: Democratic People's Republic of Korea (NK); Republic of Korea (SK)*

Capitals: Pyongyang (NK); Seoul (SK)

Official language: Korean

Official religion: None

Seoul

North Korea's flag

South Korea's flag

Korean peninsula

Year of founding:	1948
National anthems:	*A Chi Mun bin Na Ra I Gang San* ("Shine Bright, O Dawn, on This Land So Fair") (NK); *Aegukga* ("A Song of Love for the Country") (SK)
Governments:	Unitary, single-party republic (NK); unitary, multiparty republic (SK)
Chiefs of state:	Chair of the National Defense Commission (NK); president (SK)
Heads of government:	Premier (NK); president (SK)
Area:	46,540 square miles (120,538 sq km) (NK); 38,328 square miles (99,268 sq km) (SK)
Land and water borders of Korean Peninsula:	China and Russia to the north, East Sea (Sea of Japan) to the east, West Sea (Yellow Sea) to the west; Japan across the Korea Strait to the southeast. The demilitarized zone (DMZ) separates North Korea from South Korea at the 38th parallel.
Highest elevations:	Mount Baekdu, 9,003 feet (2,744 m) above sea level (NK); Mount Halla, 6,398 feet (1,950 m) above sea level (SK)
Lowest elevation:	Sea level
Average temperature extremes:	In January, 18°F (–8°C) at Pyongyang (NK) and 28°F (–2°C) at Busan (SK). In July, 75°F (24°C) in Pyongyang (NK) and 81°F (27°C) in the lowlands (SK).
Average precipitation extremes:	40 inches (100 cm) in most of North Korea; 50 inches (127 cm) in the southeast South Korea

Cheomseongdae

Currency

National populations (2002 est.):	22,224,195 (NK); 48,324,000 (SK)	
Population of largest North Korean cities:	Pyongyang (1999 est.)	3,136,000
	Nampo (1993)	731,448
	Hamheung (1993)	709,000
	Cheongjin (1993)	582,480
Population (2000) of largest South Korean cities:	Seoul	9,891,000
	Busan	3,664,000
	Daegu	2,480,000
	Incheon	2,476,000

Famous landmarks:
- ▶ *Cheomseongdae Observatory*, Gyeongju, South Korea
- ▶ *International Friendship Exhibition*, Mount Myohyang, North Korea
- ▶ *Gyongbokgung Palace*, Seoul, South Korea
- ▶ *Mount Baekdu*, northern North Korea
- ▶ *Panmunjeom*, central Korea in the DMZ
- ▶ *Seoraksan National Park*, northeastern South Korea

Industry: North Korea's main industries are the government and military. Leading manufacturing industries include cement, chemicals, iron and steel, and heavy machinery and metals. South Korea's leading industries include shipbuilding and the manufacture of automobiles, computer equipment, textiles, clothing, and shoes.

Official currency: The *won*. In June 2004, U.S. $1 = 1,165 South Korean won; U.S. $1 = 151 North Korean won.

System of weights and measures: Metric and traditional systems

Korean children

Rhee Syngman

Literacy rate: 95 percent (1997, NK); 98 percent (1998, SK)

Common Korean words and phrases:

Annyongha-simnikka. [AHN-nyong hah SIM-nik-gah]	Hello.
Annyeonghi gaseyo. [AHN-nyong-hee GAH-saeh-yoh]	Good-bye.
Cheonmaneyo. [CHON-mah-naeh-yoh]	You're welcome.
Gamsa hamnida. [GAHM-sah HAHM-nee-dah]	Thank you.
Ye. [YEH]	Yes.
Aniyo. [AH-nee-yoh]	No.
Olma imnikka? [U-mah IM-neek-gah]	How much does it cost?
Eodi iseumnigga? [UDD-ay is-SOOM-nik-gah]	Where is . . . ?

Famous Koreans:

Chung Kyung-wha (1944–)
Violinist

Jo Su-mi (1962–)
Opera singer

Kim Dae-jung (1925–)
*President of South Korea (1998–2002)
and winner of 2000 Nobel Peace Prize*

Kim Il-sung (1912–1994)
North Korea's first leader (1948–1984)

Kim Jong-il (1942–)
*Son of Kim Il-sung and
North Korea's second leader (1997–)*

Sejong (1397–1450)
*King who encouraged invention
of Korean alphabet*

Rhee Syngman (1875–1965)
*South Korea's first president
(1948–1960)*

Yi Sun-sin (1545–1598)
*Admiral and inventor of
world's first ironclad ship*

To Find Out More

Books

▶ Chun Hui-jung, Lee Hyo-gee, and Han Young-sil. *Traditional Korean Food*. Seoul: Ministry of Culture and Tourism, 2000.

▶ Clark, Donald N. *Culture and Customs of Korea*. Culture and Customs of Asia series. Westport, CT.: Greenwood Press, 2000.

▶ Dudley, William (ed.). *North and South Korea*. Opposing Viewpoints series. Farmington Hills, MI.: Greenhaven Press, 2003.

▶ Goldstein, Donald M. and Harry J. Maihafer. *The Korean War: The Story and Photographs*. Washington, D.C.: Brassey's, 2000.

▶ *Korea*. Ask About Asia series. Broomall, PA: Mason Crest Publishers, 2003.

▶ McMahon, Patricia. *Chi-Hoon: A Korean Girl*. Honesdale, PA.: Boyds Mills Press, 1993

▶ Park, Frances, and Ginger Park. *My Freedom Trip: A Child's Escape from North Korea*. Honesdale, PA.: Boyds Mills Press, 1998.

▶ Salter, Christopher L. *North Korea*. Modern World Nations series. Philadelphia: Chelsea House, 2003.

▶ Shepheard, Patricia. *South Korea*. Major World Nations series. Philadelphia: Chelsea House, 1999.

▶ *South Korea*. Festivals of the World series. Milwaukee, WI: Gareth Stevens, 1998.

▶ Won Moo Hurh. *The Korean Americans*. The New Americans series. Westport, CT.: Greenwood Press, 1998.

Video Recordings

▶ *Asia Rising—Japan and Korea Rebuild*. WGBH Boston: PBS, 1999. Second half of 60-minute video shows South Korea's rise to economic prosperity from the end of the Korean War to the early 1990s.

▶ *Families of South Korea*. Master Communication, 2001. Two 15-minute segments depicting life of two families in a village and in Seoul—meals, special occasions, school.

▶ *Hidden Korea*. PBS Home Video, 2001. A 60-minute video showcasing traditional foods, crafts, arts, and religious practices.

Web sites

▶ **Korean Central News Agency**
http://www.kcna.co.jp/index-e.htm
Web site of the state-run news agency of the Democratic People's Republic of Korea.

▶ **Korea.net: Korean Government Homepage**
http://www.korea.net/kwnews/index1.asp
Official Web site of the Korean government with links to news, the economy, culture, science, sports, and travel.

Organizations and Embassies

▶ **Republic of Korea Embassy**
1370 Massachusetts Avenue NW
Washington, D.C. 20008

▶ **Korean National Tourism Organization**
737 North Michigan Avenue
Suite 910
Chicago, IL 60611

Index

Page numbers in *italics* indicate illustrations.

Meet the Author

PATRICIA K. KUMMER writes and edits textbook materials and nonfiction books for children and young adults from her home office in Lisle, Illinois. She earned a bachelor of arts degree in history from the College of St. Catherine in St. Paul, Minnesota, and a master of arts degree in history from Marquette University in Milwaukee, Wisconsin. Before starting her career in publishing, she taught social studies at the junior high/middle-school level.

Since then, Kummer has written about American, African, Asian, and European history for textbook publishers. More recently she wrote *Côte d'Ivoire*, *Ukraine*, *Tibet*, *Singapore*, and *Cameroon* in the Children's Press series Enchantment of the World. One of her favorite projects was writing a commissioned biography for Jerry Reinsdorf, chairman of the Chicago Bulls and Chicago White Sox.

"Writing books about people, states, and countries requires a great deal of research," says Kummer. "To me, researching is the most fun part of a project. My method of research begins by going online. For this book, I found several good Web sites, many of them from departments of South Korea's government. Then I went to several nearby libraries for the most

Author with traditional Korean bride's box, celadon vases, and paper fan.

recent books on both North Korea and South Korea. To keep up with events in both countries, I signed on to a Listserv that sent me daily news reports." To appreciate Korea's traditional music, I attended a program of Intangible Cultural Properties (traditional Korean songs and dances) performed by several of Korea's Human Cultural Treasures.

"When I needed answers that I could not find in any of these sources, I e-mailed questions to the Korean Tourism Board in Chicago. I also located Americans and Korean Americans who had recently visited Korea and e-mailed questions to them about daily life. Because North Korea's government limits information about the country, it was difficult obtaining accurate, up-to-date statistics and a clear idea about the daily life of its citizens."

Kummer hopes that this book will help young people better understand the history of the Korean people and the current status of the two countries on the Korean Peninsula.

Photo Credits